The formation of a county government in Kenya

KINYANJUI NGANGA

Copyright © Kinyanjui Nganga 2011
P.O. Box 13514 – 00100
Nairobi, Kenya.

Cell: 254 721 222243 / 733 222243

Email: kinyanjui@shapeafrika.com

Website: www.shapeafrika.com

Original Nairobi edition 2011

ISBN-13:
978-1499733037

ISBN-10:
1499733038

Unsung Heroes

Let it never be forgotten that glamour is not
greatness
Applause is not fame
Prominence is not eminence
The man of the hour is not up to be the man of the
ages
A stone may spackle but that does not make it
diamond
A man may have money but that does not make
him a success

It is what the unimportant do that really count and
determine the cause of history
The greatest forces in the universe are never
spectacular
Some showers are more effective than hurricanes
but they get no publicity
The world will soon die but for the fidelity, loyalty
and consecration of those whose names are never
honoured and unsung.

Dr. Joseph Schuzu

Acknowledgements

Timeless acknowledgements to the heroes of this country who bled and died for our independence; some of whom never lived to see the light of *Uhuru*. Your sacrificial efforts will never be forgotten as long as this country endures.

Sincere appreciation to the country's leadership that has faithfully carried on the legacy mantle of our freedoms.

Special acknowledgement is tossed to H.E. the President of Kenya, Hon Mwai Kibaki, for his dedicated leadership in the country's quest for a new constitution. Passionate appreciation to the Right Honorable Prime Minister, Hon Raila Odinga, for his forthright and decisive leadership in our country's search for a people driven constitutional order.

Ultimate acknowledgement to the One and Only True God and source of Eternal life upon whom the successful implementation of Kenya's new constitutional order directly depend. To Him alone, be all the Glory whenever the proposals in this volume are read and practiced.

Acronyms and abbreviations

ADHEK   –   Association of Developing Horticultural Exporters of Kenya

AU   –   African Union

CDF   –   Constituency Development Funds

CID   –   Criminal Investigation Department

DRC   –   Democratic Republic of Congo

EAC   –   East Africa Community

ECOWAS   –   Economic Community of West African States

EU   –   European Union

FORD   –   Forum for Restoration of Democracy

FPEAK   –   Fresh Produce Export Association of Kenya

GDP   –   Gross Domestic Product

HE   –   His Excellency

HR   –   Human Resource

ICC	–	International Criminal Court
IDP	–	Internally Displaced Person
IT	–	Information Technology
IEBC	–	Independent Electoral and Boundaries Commission
IIEC	–	Interim Independent Electoral Commission
IIBRC	–	Interim Independent Boundaries Review Commission
KACA	–	Kenya Anti Corruption Authority
KAU	–	Kenya African Union
KADU	–	Kenya African Democratic Union
KANU	–	Kenya African National Union
KENHA	–	Kenya Highway Authority
KeRRA	–	Kenya Rural Roads Authority
KPU	–	Kenya People's Union
KRC	–	Kenya Red Cross
KURA	–	Kenya Urban Roads Authority
LEGCO	–	Legislative Council

NARC	–	National Alliance Rainbow Coalition
NCEC	–	National Convention Executive Council
NCPC	–	National Convention Planning Committee
NEMA	–	National Environmental Management Authority
ODM	–	Orange Democratic Movement
PEV	–	Post Election Violence
PNU	–	Party of National Unity
PPOA	–	Public Procurement Oversight Authority
PRC	–	People's Republic of China
PS	–	Permanent Secretary
SPV	–	Special Purpose Vehicle
UAE	–	United Arab Emirates
UN	–	United Nations
TJRC	–	Truth Justice & Reconciliation Commission
WFP	–	World Food Program

Definitions of Terms

Harambee – President Kenyatta's philosophy of working together

Matatu – Public Transport Vehicles

Mlolongo – Queuing system

Mwananchi – Citizen

Mzee – Old Man

Nyama Choma – Roasted Beef

Nyayo – President Moi's philosophy: In Mzee's footsteps

Saba Saba – July Seventh (Saba means Seven)

Serikari – Government

Siri Kari – Great Secret

Ugali – Traditional food made from maize flour

Uhuru – Independence

Wananchi – Citizens

CONTENTS

DEDICATION

Dedicated to the constituents of the 47 counties in Kenya whom I desire to challenge as well as inspire to arise to the new constitutional order. May each county in Kenya form a government model whose success could be replicated countrywide and scaled up throughout our beautiful continent of Africa towards the realization of the Millennial Development Goals.

Introduction

Principles of success are universal at individual, family, institutional, corporate, county, national or global levels. Evidently, the public sector has of late undertaken to benchmark with the private sector in many of its operations. This recipe has been the birth of the rapid results initiative of the government. The author stresses the need for governing the county governments in a similar manner like one would do for a private enterprise without compromising on social responsibilities that would be too exorbitant if left at the mercy of approaching all sectors from a profit point of view.

Individuals are known to pay almost any price for private gain. If works along public utilities were perceived with the same attitudes by the custodians of respective offices, then the growth rate of devolved government would be phenomenal. From the author's perspective, the country has enough resources to overtake the so called `Asian Giants' under this new constitutional order if the right attitudes, approaches and virtues of work were embraced across all counties.

Each county should be competitive, innovative and creative enough to attract investors, educate as well as provide security and health care to its constituents. Each county is economically viable and can be self sustaining and be able to borrow and led on its own name with tangible collaterals as an enterprise. Healthy competition should be encouraged amongst the counties to enhance development whilst the national government takes care of the national resources. However, healthy social-economic competition amongst counties should never compromise our oneness. As the dictum on the United States seal states, *Epluribus*

Unum, out of many, one. Originating from all corners of the world, the Americans chose to unite as one people – a spirit we ought to embrace in the new constitutional dispensation.

The original vision of the Father Founders of our nation was a country free of poverty, disease and illiteracy. This well intended dream was however thwarted by selfish driven governance coupled with leadership ignorance on the posterity impact. We must never go back to such a quagmire that has unfortunately bred gross corruption, insecurity, intolerance, tribal animosity, disease, ignorance and untold poverty. High levels of hunger and a sense of hopelessness lingers in many parts of the country which ought to be in the sea of forgetfulness in this time and age.

The ills in our country can largely be contributed to a wrong start. Prior to the first election of independent Kenya in 1968, the constitution had been illegally amended and skewed to suit the interests of the minority at the expense of the majority. This book attempts to emphasize the need to form a people-accountable county government that is not only transparent but also answerable to the people it serves. The *siri-kari* attitude of public service must be aborted even before it is birthed in the county governments. The County Assemblies must be run in the full light of the public they seek to serve with only restricting the public from any sensitive debate that can compromise the security of the county.

The suggestions herein seek to inform the successful formation of a model county government. However, it's the responsibility of each county government to see what works for their specific needs. Thus the proposals in this book should be seen as suggestions rather than canon laws that must be followed as spelt out herein. Nevertheless, the thoughts shared are universal principally and are meant to make a worthy contribution in the country's new constitutional order.

This book first traces the constitutional journey and the price the country had to pay to reach the new constitutional dispensation. Those who fought for more inclusive governance and their respective contributions are acknowledged with precision. Then the writer seeks to elucidate on the implications of the new constitutional order in real life situations. This is meant to help the reader see the relevance of the new constitution if various fields of endeavor and how it affects one's individual, family and corporate life from the previous constitutional order.

The book then seeks to challenge every county to have a distinct identity upon which it can take competitive advantage economically and socially. Lessons from our history, successes and failures, are closely examined to help advice future governance at the county level. Ignoring historical lessons can lead to replica of our past mistakes. To this end, the author draws several parallels from our history with current happenings to shed meaningful light on how we can break from our yester ills. This can only be practical through servant-hood leadership at the county levels that inspire vision and stir development. The writer thus takes great page addressing the characteristics of servant leadership picturing the local context.

This volume does a comparative analysis between the devolved governance structures spelt out in our new constitution with similar ones across the world. Failures and successes are both studied in an attempt to benchmark in the formation of our county governments. The idea of prioritizing issues in the county government is equally given a lot of weight since resources, human and capital, are never adequate to meet all the desired goals immediately. Succession leadership is explored and ways

3

of passing on the mantle successfully by mentoring incoming leaders who will respect ongoing projects is emphasized. This is especially because in times past, projects have been sacrificed at the altar of political supremacy by successive leadership.

Finally, the author speaks of setting the systems right from the word go rather than embracing a fire fighting reactive leadership style rushing from one crisis to another. This leads to appointments of various commissions to investigate misuse of public funds, abuse of office, loss of lives and myriad other catastrophes due to lack of principled guidelines. When systems are vague or non-existence, issues become personalized. Responsible leadership foresees and prepares accordingly for any eventualities. If the county governments set their financial, procurement, security, project management and resource allocations systems from the very onset, constituents will not be over bothered with who runs the county – since such public officers will be but be implementers of already existing systems.

Setting strong systems is the surest way of reaching the Promised Land by our new constitution. This is so because people change and can distort and take advantage of un-laid down procedures for selfish personal interests that protect the greed of monopoly at the expense of the majority. When we are guided by structures that give opportunities to the small scale farmer and business owner, politicking in all street corners of this country will cease and the populace will embark on personal growth and national development. Then and only then can we reach in our time and for all times, peace on earth and goodwill toward all men.

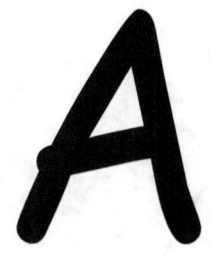 Smooth Sail

Never Made a Skilled Mariner

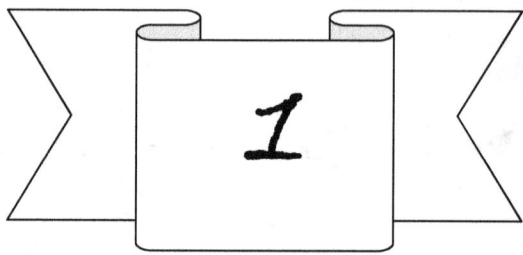

<u>The Constitutional Sail</u>

Undoubtedly the most momentous and sublime event since our country's declaration of independence was the promulgation of our new constitution on August the 27th 2010 after a successful referendum process held on the 4th of the same month. From the Interim Independent Electoral Commission of Kenya (IIEC) final count, 6,092,593 Kenyans voted `Yes' while 2,795,059 Kenyans voted `No' to the gleaming new constitution. Any objective observer of our country's history must acknowledge that this was a clear indication that the Kenyan people wanted a break from the past constitutional order. Indeed even the `No' voters agreed that the constitution was by and large a great document save for a few clauses whose consensus was never reached.

Perhaps in slightly less than a thousand years consensus would have been achieved by angelic aliens driving the constitutional debate! Thanks to God indeed that the majority saw the light of this intuitive truth and took the bold step of voting into the greatest governance positive change witnessed anywhere. Interestingly enough, both sides of the constitutional voting divide agreed that the promulgation of the new constitution was a re-birth of our country.

Skeptics however may want us to believe that the voters just followed their tribal kingpins blindly without ever perusing through the previously draft constitution under contest. I will desist from this sort of argument and stick to the issue before hand. The constitution has been overwhelmingly passed, period. A new dawn has risen for Kenya. This act of courage could have salvaged the toppling of our government as witnessed in Tunisia and Egypt early this year through mass protests. The quest for a new constitution was wearing the people down and the country's patience was being exhausted. So, where did this journey begin?

A Smooth Sail Never Made a Skilled Mariner
The constitution making process was not any easy sail. It was never meant to be in anyway. Anything given for free is valued for nothing. No wonder we trod upon the first constitution with ease since its very object was to rush into an emergency: Independence! Thus the negotiators never really engaged themselves in the making of a very workable document.

The initial attempt to the successful promulgation of our constitution perhaps can be traced back to 1952 when a state of emergency was declared due to the uprising resistance to the oppressive colonial white rule. 183 Kenya African Union (KAU) leaders were arrested with the famous Kapenguria 6 charged in the notorious trial with managing the proscribed society of Mau

Mau. The detention of these brave nationalists: Jomo Kenyatta, Paul Ngei, Achieng Oneko, Bildad kaggia, Fred Kubai and Kung'u Karumba intensified the war of liberation making Kenya and Algeria the two African colonies to wage a bloody insurgency against settler colonialism.

Events unfolded and the colonialists began to feel the heat of the native resistance to the domineering by the minority on the basis of their colour pigmentation. In 1958, all the 14 elected African members of the Legislative Council (LEGCO) walked out of the chambers when Governor Evelyn Baring insisted on zero constitutional amendments. This was in reference to the colonial constitution that governed Kenya. Notwithstanding, law talks began in 1960 and continued gaining momentum through subsequent years between 1961 and 1963. This birthed the Lancaster house Constitutional Conference held in London and Nairobi in 1963 to negotiate Kenya's independence constitution.

With the promulgation of Kenya's independence constitution, the colonialists felt safe enough and their interests largely guarded and thus were ready to relinquish power. In May 1963, general elections were held on the principle of one person, one vote. The Kenya African national Union (KANU) obtained thunderous victory and Kenya attained internal self-government on June 1st of the same year. On December the 12th 1963, full independence was granted to Kenya after 61 years of colonial rule. On that most eventful and emotive moment, the nation's first Prime Minister, Mzee Jomo Kenyatta, rose from his seat and strode in step with the Duke of Edinburgh to an elevated position 10 meters from the stage. The flag of the British Empire was lowered for the last time and, to strains of the young nation's anthem, a new flag fluttered in its place when the floodlights came back on that night of December 12, 1963.

On the self same date in 1964, Kenya became a republic with Jomo Kenyatta as the first president after unification of hitherto dual executive. KANU and the opposition party, Kenya African Democratic Union (KADU) merged to pave way for de facto one party system. This could have been the genesis of disrespect to the constitution evidently witnessed with the assassination of charismatic politician, Pio Gama Pinto outside his Nairobi residence in 1965. The country's first vice president entered another logger head phase with the presidency and founded an opposition party, the Kenya People's Union (KPU). However, this was short lived as the party was banned and its leaders detained following the assassination of Tom Mboya in 1969, a powerful cabinet minister and KANU's secretary general then.

A constitutional amendment made Kenya a de jure one party state to forestall the registration of an opposition political party by Jaramogi Oginga Odinga and George Moseti Anyona in 1982. In August 1 of the same year, Kenya experienced perhaps the darkest hour of its existence as an attempted coup d'etat was ruthlessly crushed by loyalist soldiers. This led to protracted crackdown on Mwakenya and other political dissidents by President Moi's regime between the years 1982 and 1988. During this time, several renowned politicians were rigged out through the infamous and notorious *mlolongo* (queue-voting) system during general elections.

In 1990, popular foreign affairs minister, Robert Ouko was assassinated which was closely related with the *Saba Saba* demonstrations. This new outfit whose central demand was a resumption of multiparty politics led to the killing of many protestors and harming including maiming of thousands. Then ruling party, KANU consequently established a Review Committee to collect views on how the party should be reformed. Meanwhile politically instigated ethnic clashes left about 1000

9

Kenyans dead and thousands displaced between 1991 and 1993 forcing donors to withdraw budgetary support.

These events led to the repeal of Section 2A of the constitution which then restored multi party politics in Kenya. The Forum for the Restoration of Democracy (FORD) held its first legal opposition rally in 22 years with the sole objective of removing President Moi from power. In December of 1992, the first multi party general election was held and the divided opposition lost to the ruling party with Kenneth Matiba's FORD-Asili becoming second, Mwai Kibaki's DP being third and Jaramogi Ondinga's FORD-Kenya being fourth.

The reality of the need for a new constitution was now recognized by the opposition strongly at this point especially to level the electioneering grounds. In 1995's New Year eve, President Moi promised a new Constitution before end year. The goal was never realized. In 1996, the National Convention Planning Committee (NCPC), the executive arm of pro-democracy forces coming together to agitate for constitutional change was formed. In 1997, the National Convention Assembly and its executive arm, the National Convention Executive Council (NCEC) were formed. Between May and July, widespread mass action forced the government to concede to minimum constitutional and legal changes necessary to facilitate freer and fairer elections. The Constitution of Kenya Review Commission Act, 1997 was passed to provide a framework for constitutional change.

Regrettably, the country witnessed the second generation of politically instigated ethnic clashes between 1998 and 1999 perhaps meant to discourage constitutional review efforts. During this period, negotiations between civil society and the political class for the review of the Constitution of Kenya Review Commission Act, 1997 led to an amendment of the act via the

Constitution of Kenya Review Commission (Amendment) Act 1998 which is now called the Constitution of Kenya Review Act, 1997 meant to be a people driven process in Constitution making. President Moi assented to the Act against a KANU parliamentary caucus that sought to exclude the civil society from the Constitutional review Act.

A resolution was passed in 1999 by parliament to establish a 27 Member Select Committee led by Raila Odinga to review the Constitution of Kenya Review Act to be in line with the wishes of the majority of the Kenyan people. The Review team which whose technocrat membership was led by Prof Yash Pal Ghai was scuttled after the 2002 elections were called upon. The ruling party since independence, KANU, was given a landslide defeat by the National Alliance Rainbow Coalition (NARC).

In his inaugural address, the NARC leader, President Kibaki promised to deliver a new constitution in 100 days. History may judge this promise harshly for a government whose elections were pegged on constitutional and institutional reforms. By and large, this promise was broken down by the collapse of the Bomas Constitutional Review talks due to the government divisions between the years 2003 and 2004. The Bomas draft was then amended to enhance the presidential powers under the chairmanship of Attorney General, Amos Wako in Kilifi. This document was then subjected to the country's first referendum and it was grossly rejected by Kenyans.

As has been our tradition, the referendum ushered the country into the succession politics of 2007 whose outcome of the general elections were sharply disputed between H.E. Mwai Kibaki's Party of National Unity (PNU) and H.E. Raila Ondinga's Orange Democratic Party (ODM) throwing the country into untold tantrums. Lives were lost and families displaced. The

11

International community stepped into the scene to mediate a peace deal between the contesting parties forming a grand coalition government with H.E. Mwai Kibaki being the president and H.E. Raila Ondinga becoming the country's Prime Minister. Agenda 4 on the peace accord witnessed by H.E. Kofi Annan, former U.N. chief, outlined necessary national reforms best epitomized into constitutional reforms.

The two national leaders committed themselves to deliver a new constitution to end the likelihood of bloodshed as witnessed in the contested 2007 Presidential elections. Parliament adopted the draft constitution as prepared by the Committee of Experts led by Nzamba Kitonga in 2010. The draft Constitution was then subjected into a referendum on the 4th of August 2010 and was adopted after being endorsed by an overwhelming majority of Kenyans. 23 days later, the President promulgated the endorsed constitution into law ushering Kenya into a New Constitutional Order on Friday the 27th August 2010 amid pomp and fanfare. Certainly, the constitutional sail has been rough, very rough, but a smooth sail never made a skilled mariner.

Lest we forget: The two most fundamental issues that agitated for a constitutional make over in Kenya were the powers of the Presidency and governance. Kenyans were frustrated by an all-powerful and manipulative presidency and at the same time sought equitable distribution of the national cake through devolved governance structures. Intuitively, there were other various reasons that called for constitutional reforms including the land policy reforms, sealing loopholes of meddling with the constitution at the whim of a minority elite class and human rights issues now elaborated in the Bill of Rights.

Whereas it is the responsibility of religious leaders to uphold the moral values of the society, the debatable clauses on abortion and

Kadhi courts emerged much later in the quest for a new constitution. We however cannot and should not see the church as an impediment to the journey towards our new constitution. We must appreciate that is the church's prerogative to defend the Christian faith and values; indeed, had the church leaders agreed wholly with all aspects of the constitution, perhaps many Kenyans would have questioned their moral standing. Thus, the goodwill that was behind these clauses must also be upheld and respected as we win the church over towards a new constitutional dispensation.

It is my constitute effort to win one and all towards rebuilding the reborn Kenya especially those who voted 'No' due to a few disturbing clauses. As we all agree, constitution making is a give and take participatory process; which as a democratic nation we have finally agreed to have the majority have their way as the minority have their say. As one nation, one people, let us forge ahead with renewed vitality, hope and determination to off load the dark ills of yesterday and to focus our sight and energies to a brighter tomorrow. Then and only then can we achieve structural peace for all Kenyans in the spirit of good neighborliness and brotherhood.

The main dangers in this life are the people who want to change everything or nothing - Lady Nancy Astor

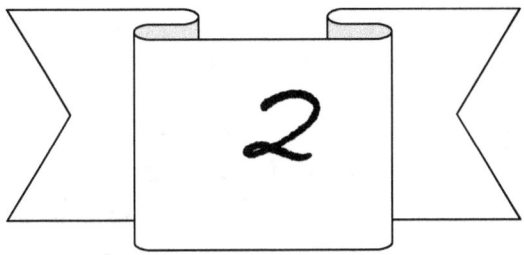

The New Constitutional Order

From the conflict theory as advanced by Karl Marx (1867), tension is the driving force behind social change. Conflict theorists see society as made up of parts that are in a constant state of conflict. C Wright Mills introduced the idea of the "power elite" – a tiny minority group of government, military and business people – who control the affairs of the nations. It is this elitist attitude towards the people that has caused a governance revolution in Tunisia and Egypt. Had the presidency and its cohorts never taken the populace for granted, perhaps the Kenyan citizenry wouldn't have agitated for a new constitutional order.

Time and again it has been said that the only constant thing in life is change. Again it has been said that if you don't change, change will change you. There is some validity to that observation. The world is very different now than it was during our independence. Successful adaptation to change is as crucial within an organization as it is in the natural world. Just like plants and animals, organizations and the individuals in them inevitably encounter changing conditions that they are powerless to control. The more effectively you deal with change, the more likely you are to thrive. Adaptation might involve establishing a structured methodology for responding to changes in the business environment (such as a fluctuation in the economy, or a threat from a competitor) or establishing coping mechanisms for responding to changes in the workplace (such as new policies, or technologies).

The universal forces of change are taking place whether consciously or unconsciously and Kenya hasn't been isolated either. I wonder however whether there could be people out there who are still struggling to comprehend what has really changed in Kenya with the promulgation of the new constitutional order in Kenya that has revolutionalized all spheres of our social economic order. Many fundamental issues have radically re-ordered Kenya's structures in diverse aspects. Most notable changes in the new constitutional order are:

New Governance Order: For the first time ever, Kenya has a devolved form of government as opposed to the centralized governance system we are used to as clearly spelt out in Chapter 11. Governance has been taken closer to the people whereby the Counties will form their own governments as indicated in Cap 11, Part 2 Clause 176. At the national level, the constitution separates executive leadership from legislative duties as cabinet secretaries will be technocrats having no political seats (Clause 152 (3)). At the county level, the county shall have a legislative arm (Clause 178) and an executive arm (Clause 179). The former may receive and approve plans and policies for management and development in the county (Clause 185 (4)) while the latter will implement, manage and coordinate county policies (Clause 183) under the leadership of an elected county governor.

Thus, the county government being based where the people are has higher chances of enhancing accountability since the leadership is more accessible and reachable by the people than the central government. Moreover, the county governor can be removed from the office (Clause 181) due to violation of the constitution, crime, gross misconduct or incapacity to perform the functions of the office of the county governor. This new constitutional framework brings governance closer to the people and once the constituents are educated properly on their role in checking the county leadership; national development goals will be reached more effectively.

Those still harboring dreams of possibilities of retaining the functions of the provincial administration are certainly on the wrong side of history and might need to take a few practical classes of civic education. Even the very retention of a restructured provincial administration in the current constitution was an ill advised political exchange. The legal governance framework rests with the county and national government; no intermediaries. Period. All reforms have a cost implication. We can't retain an obsolete administrative structure to safeguard jobs for political cause. At the meantime, as it were, the Provincial administration will remain as employees of the national government strictly respecting the devolved structures.

Article 17 of the new constitution provides that: `Within five years after the effective date, the national government shall restructure the system of administration commonly known as the Provincial Administration to accord with and respect the system of devolved government established under this constitution'. Some obsolete minded politicians wish to interpret this statement grammatically ignoring multiple realities surrounding the spirit of the new constitution. The constitutional change was driven, by and large, by an equivocal craving to dismantle the insidious executive powers and disperse them to the grassroots. Governance is now premised on inclusivity as decided by the indefatigable sovereign will of the Kenyan people.

New Political Order: The constitution reforms the political structure in many ways including the introduction of 2 Chamber Houses of Parliament (Cap 8, Part 1); enhancing voting transparency and resolving electoral disputes (Cap 7, Part 1); recognizing independent candidates (Clause 99©); setting a specific electioneering date (Clause 136 (2)) and swearing in timeframes (Clause 141) and devolving the powers of the Presidency to consult in decision making processes and in all public appointments. The real separation of powers between the three arms of government: executive, legislature and judiciary brings a new scale of political check and balances that will propel this country into our dream of being a middle income earner among the family of nations.

The old dirty politics of rigging out leaders during party nominations will be greatly checked since candidates have the option of seeking votes independently.   This will enhance democratic nominations at party level to retain a high caliber of leaders. The election dates which were traditionally used by the presidency as secret political weapons giving undue advantage to the incumbent will be a thing of the past. Leaders can now prepare and plan for their political careers adequately making elective appointments genuinely competitive in acquisition of the best in class.

Women, the youth and disadvantaged groups as well as minorities of all kinds are deliberately considered in the management of the country both at the national and county (Clause 177 (1)(b)(c)) levels. Thus the constitution as it is embraces multiple realities in the society. This will include people who otherwise due to financial and myriad other limitations would never have a chance to present their unheard interests. The ability to recall non performing public officers (Clause 181) will raise the accountability levels of the county governments. Bearing the fact that the country will definitely have an economic boom and competitive jobs will be readily available for the qualified, anyone seeking an elective position will do so purely to serve the people. That is, of course, if the people rise up to the occasion and keep their leaders in the right frame of service mind as anticipated in the new constitution.

Many of our leaders have been selfless and sincere in their public service. A few though entered politics for monetary gains and when they do not know how long their political careers will last, they engage in voracious graft. Since the political class at the national level will not be heading the ministries, opportunities for ill gotten wealth will immensely be reduced. What a joy to live in these interesting times to witness a new political dispensation in Kenya. We must selflessly guard against losing so hard fought battles for cheap political gains.

New Public Finance Order: Public funds will be devolved into the county levels (Clause 202 (1) (2)) and the treasury's grip on the country's kitty is loosed as funds will be controlled by two new offices: The Office of the Commissioner for Revenue

Allocations (Clause 215 (1-4)) which will determine the sharing of revenues between the central government and the devolved administration and the Office of the Controller of the Budget (Cap 12, Part 7, Clause 228) which will be in charge of overseeing the execution of the budget. The wide and discretionary powers that the treasury has been enjoying originate from the fact that it can alter budgetary allocations mid-year ignoring the parliamentary approved budget. This has adversely affected national economic policies. This has extensively being addressed in the entire chapter 12 of our constitution which details the principles and framework of public finance (Part 1); other public funds (Part 2); revenue-raising powers and public debt (Part 3); revenue allocation (Part 4); budgets and spending (Part 5); control of public money (Part 6) and financial officers and institutions (Part 7).

The people at the county level can now set goals and prioritize on issues that directly contribute to the welfare of the county like security, education, health, agriculture, entrepreneurship, entertainment, infrastructures etc. areas of development that were ignored at times unconsciously by the centralized system of government can no longer be put aside in the waste basket. The national government in a large way has been determining areas of priority for the country in an un-equitable manner locking out the regions perceived unproductive like northern Kenya. An educated assessment at countries with dominating desert climate proves to Kenya that developing any given place on this earth is a matter of choice and every region is incredibly resourceful and significant to national growth.

Lots of mangoes for export are grown in North Eastern counties which the central government had overlooked in afore time in many development agenda. This will be past as these beloved Kenyans arise to show casing their potential and I foresee some counties will surprise the so-perceived potent ones in less than a decade from the writing of this book. These are counties whose constituents will not complain on what they do not have but will maximally make use of what they do have. They will embrace accountability, goal setting and servitude in their leadership style for the benefit of their brotherhood.

New Social Order: The new constitutional order affects the lives of the Kenyan citizenry dynamically. For instance, our brothers and sisters in the diasporas are overly excited that acquisition of foreign citizenship will no longer make a citizen by birth lose his/her Kenyan citizenship (Clause 16). One major implication of this aspect of our law is that the new social order encourages investing at home while working abroad.

Moreover, all state organs and all public officers have the duty to address the needs of vulnerable groups within society, including women, older members of society, persons with disabilities, children, youth, members of minority or marginalized communities, and members of particular ethnic, religious or cultural communities (Clause 21 (3)). Trusting that in the light of this part of the law and incorporating the devolved structure of government; the communities in the Northern and North Eastern regions of Kenya will no longer be unduly marginalized.

It is good news to note that no fee may be charged for commencing proceedings in a court of law when the rights of individuals are denied, violated or infringed, or are threatened (Clause 22 (3) ©). Pursuit of justice for all has never been made more real and reachable. Besides, every person has the right of access to information held by the state (Clause 35(1)). The actualization of this specific right is subject to prove in practice, though. This is especially so whereby the State deliberately chooses to conceal information in the disguise of national security. Though partially acceptable as a global practice, the public must guard against this secrecy theorem to drive us back to the dark eras of our leadership characterized by torture of people in Nyayo house dungeons.

Many more aspects revolutionalizing the social order include the expansion of environmental and social rights, labour relations and especially allowing formation of trade unions across all organizations, respect and preservation of cultural values and languages, equal rights of spouses in marriage and rights of arrested persons. Women in particular are great beneficiaries of the new constitutional order not only in leadership positions but also in the formation, life and dissolution of marriage (Clause 45 (3)). Objectively analyzing the new social order with a hawk's eye sheds the light that multiple realities have been comprehensively incorporated to guard the fundamental rights of children, persons living with disabilities, senior citizens and minority groups. The county governments must operate under these guiding principles to make sense of a progressive governance approach of our society.

New Legal Order: Today in our mortal hands is a constitution that can be altered at the mere whelm of a small group in parliamentary chambers. This is profound. We can now work out government structures, frameworks and policies confidently knowing clearly that our plans cannot be distorted for political gains or under any intimidation of whatever sort. The independent constitution was amended without seeking Kenyans permission; in any case, they were never consulted during its writing. The supremacy of the constitution rests with the people of Kenya and thus I encourage all constituents of Kenya, wherever they may be to get on with their respective county development plans *asap.*

A great deviation from the past is the judicial outlook and the entire legal framework. Our judges are differentially called "My Lords" and magistrates "Your Honour" by people they perceive as their serfs. Wearing red or black medieval robes, they have a scaring look that suggests prejudgment and chose to use incomprehensible language to ordinary consumers and their decisions utterly unpredictable even when the law is as clear as day and night. Justice has a monetary tag and thus subverted with ease to suppress the poor who cannot afford to buy it. This place otherwise of refugee is a haven of torture abhorred by the Kenyan commoner. Little attention was paid to the veracity of allegations against the accused. There was no threshold of culpability to protect the innocent from preying enemies.

We have had Attorney Generals who hardly prosecute leaders involved with graft. We are still harboring the ghosts of Goldenberg and Agro-leasing related scandals among thousands of others and the victims are enjoying themselves in their palatial homes and vast but unfairly acquired investments. At the same time, the courts have lost public trust over the years. We thus invite this new constitutional dispensation with great expectation coupled with a sigh of relief that justice that will not exhort the poor and defend the rich while in the wrong. Justice that upholds the constitution has finally arrived. The judges will undergo rigorous vetting and appointments will no longer be personal deals cut in the local exclusive lounges in the not so common hotels.

The Kenya Anti Corruption Authority will be a great gainer of the constitutional order and will flex its muscles of justice on graft with sure results. Of keen interest is to reiterate the fact that a

Judicial Service Commission is established (Clauses 171 and 172) which shall promote and facilitate the independence and accountability of the Judiciary and the efficient, effective and transparent administration of justice. Judges will be appointed competitively in very transparent manner. The composition of the commission makes it almost impractical to compromise its leadership which will finally make sense of the words of our National Anthem: Justice be our Shield and Defender. This commission will appoint, receive complaints against, investigate and remove from office or otherwise discipline registrars, magistrates, other Judicial officers and other staff of the Judiciary (Clause 172 (1) ©). No longer will cases have a back log in our courts since non performance will not be condoned. With the New Judicial Order in Kenya, what more can we ask to facilitate national and personal growth and development? Kenya will never be the same again but it will be the responsibilities of the ordinary *mwananchi* to enhance the system works right from the onset.

New Land policies Order: Land is the natural heritage bestowed upon us as a country with the resources therein. This natural resource has been a bone of contention at community as well as domestic levels in Kenya. One of our greatest challenges in Kenya is not really the lack and/or misuse of our natural resources. The real tragedy in this nation is failure to utilize optimally our human resources. We use up nature's natural resources by using them up while we use up man's natural resources by not making use of them at all. The New Constitutional dispensation digresses to a great extent from the independence constitution in many ways.

The most interesting aspect of land policy in my opinion is in Cap 5 Part 1, Clause 60 that says land in Kenya shall be held, used and managed in a manner that is equitable, productive and sustainable, and in accordance with the principles of equitable access to land, security of land rights, sustainable and productive management of land resources, transparent and cost effective administration of land, sound conservation and protection of ecology sensitive areas, elimination of gender discrimination in law, customs and practices related to land and property in land.

The implication is that the county governments must ensure that all land is utilized productively for the gain of the entire county and in an equitable manner amongst the constituents. This policy should not only eliminate idle land holding but also the huge gap that has existed between landlords and tenants in Kenya's history. Besides, parliament will enact laws to prescribe minimum and maximum land holding acreages in respect of private land (Clause 68 © (i)).Water catchments like Lake Naivasha are public lands (Cap 5, Part 1, Clause 62 (g)) and should not be unfairly used up and drain the conservation at the expense of many to profit a selected few sacred cows. Moreover, land ownership by non citizens has been limited to 99 years (Clause 65 (2)).

The county governments shall hold land in trust of their constituents and shall be administered on their behalf by the national Land Commission for land classified under Clause 62 (2). The county governments can broaden their economic ventures through `county lands' for the benefit of their constituents and for improving ecological aspects of their county. For instance, if every county makes a deliberate effort to ensure that all land, private or public, through a county by-law has minimum forest coverage, the entire nation would turn green and combat the forces of climate change. It's much easier to green Kenya through piece meal county efforts than by attempting to handle the entire country wholesale.

Winning everyone to embrace the New Constitutional Order
The concerns raised by the church that led her to vehemently oppose the new constitution were founded on fundamental principles and cannot be wished away so easily without due consideration. In his December 12th 2010 Daily nation article, Dean and SUNY Distinguished Professor, Makau Mutua argues that the Constitution protects gays. He cites Section 27 (1) of the 'equal protection' and the fact that the constitution does not out-rightly prohibit same-sex acts and is silent on same-sex marriages. Moreover, Section 27 (4) provides that no one will be discriminated against on grounds of sex. He even has the audacity to declare Sections 162 – 165 of the Penal code that criminalizes same-sex acts as unconstitutional.

I do not wish to engage the brutally writing distinguished professor at all but at least he confirms what the church feared against the lying assurances by the political class on this subject. The same arguments can be extended to the whole debate on abortion. One can argue that since Section 26 (4) states that abortion is not permitted; it is not illegal, per se. All moralists, irrespective of religion, color or political persuasion have issues with these moral concerns. Some of us decided not to throw away the baby with the bath water trusting to garner enough muscles after the promulgation of the constitution to repeal these specific moral concerns which may only be reflecting the values of the minority in Kenya.

There is thus the need to reach out to all Kenyans to embrace the new dawn. The new constitutional order elucidates light in all walks of life and not limited just by those highlighted above. The changes presented by the new constitutional are many more beyond the luxury of time and space for analysis purposes. Whereas most of these changes contribute very positively to the society in diverse ways, resistance to change is an inevitable human practice. Most people are comfortable with familiar grounds and resist ambiguity or venturing into new systems and lifestyles. Effective handling of such resistance to adopting the spirit of the new constitution is fundamental for the country's success.

People resist change due to various reasons like the risk of change is seen as greater than the risk of standing still; People feel connected to other people who are identified with the old way; People have no role models for the new activity; People fear they lack the competence to change; People feel overloaded and overwhelmed; People have a healthy skepticism and want to be sure new ideas are sound; People fear hidden agendas among would-be reformers; People feel the proposed change threatens their notions of themselves; People anticipate a loss of status or quality of life; and some People genuinely believe that the proposed change is a bad idea.

To overcome fears related with the adoption and implementation of the new constitutional order, the country's leadership especially the parliamentary select committee, that is, the Constitutional Implementation Oversight Committee and the Commission for the Implementation of the Constitution stipulated in the Sixth Schedule Clauses 4 and 5 respectively should manage the change in proven and workable mannerisms. For instance, as much as it is within hands, the leadership should encourage public Participation; clear communication; appoint change champions; make public the Timetable for implementing various changes; copy examples of good practice; recruit expertise in change management; change items incrementally and consider a pathfinder change programme first.

We ought to board as many people as humanly possible towards the acceptance of the new constitutional change that has taken place to have a national goodwill. It is upon this goodwill that the foundations of change will remain unshakeable. Oft times there is a temptation with leaders to ignore proper implementation of change and resolve arrogantly that `whoever boards, boards; whoever is left out, is left out. Shape up or ship out!' The new constitutional dispensation calls for an attitudinal change in our leadership approach to accommodate divergent schools of thought in a democratic and modern society. So, let us care enough to sell this auspicious document with humility in the spirit of national pride and genuine conviction to our county members in a language they understand best.

From psychosocial approaches in education as advanced by the Brazilian scholar, Paulo Freire, whenever development is imposed on the people, it is rejected, opposed and destroyed. True and sustainable development is like a tree. It must fit local conditions, grow from bottom up, be driven by the locals as well as implemented by the beneficiaries. Lots of well intended development projects by various development agencies end up hitting a snag because of being driven by outsiders. Thus, we must win everyone into this new found freedom for our development agenda to be sustainable. This can be done through rigorous civic education by experts well versed with andragogical training methodologies.

As President Kibaki said it in August 27, 2010, "The new constitution gives us renewed optimism about our country and its future. As young leaders, we envisioned turning our newly born country into prosperous, healthy and developed nation in a generation or two. A lot has been achieved towards this goal, but much more work remains to be done. The new constitution gives our nation a historic opportunity to decisively conquer the challenges that face us today. It provides us an avenue to renew our fight against unemployment and poverty; an opportunity to work and become a developed people and nation. I appeal to Kenyans, individually and collectively, to build a nation that will socially and economically be inclusive and cohesive where all have equal access and opportunities."

As Mr. President rightly observed, much of what was envisioned has not been achieved. We ought to work not to reach at such a disappointment years on. While presiding over the independence celebrations 47 years ago, Prince Phillip said, "The pages of (the) volume (of Kenya's independence) are still blank and empty; the story to be written is still in the hands and hearts and minds of the people of Kenya. Together as one nation, you can get rid of poverty, ignorance and disease … You can prove to the world it is possible for people of different races and creeds to live together in one country in peace and harmony"

We have been divided all the more, not against racial background, but against tribal lines. The consequences of the tribal animosity witnessed in Kenya are better never reiterated. But together in the light of the new constitution, we can begin a new, have a rejuvenated start and embrace one another once more. We are well able to bury the hatchet and turn our economy into vibrancy with sustained double-digit growth rates. We can eradicate or at least greatly minimize crime, ignorance, hate, disease and poverty in the wake of the new constitutional order. Let us awake with revived vitality, renewed hope, determined faith and dedicated focus and forge ahead full speed to usher this long awaited new dawn.

It is not the strongest species that survive, nor the most intelligent, but the ones who are most responsive to change - Charles Darwin

The County Identity

The After studying 8 previous civilizations, Oswald Spengler (1918) defined 5 stages in the life of a society, namely, birth, childhood, maturity (the golden age), decline (old age) and death. Each stage must be navigated successfully prior to graduating to the next one, he posed. I see Kenya in her golden age which he refers to as generative, a process by which persons guide the oncoming generation or make efforts to improve the society in a meaningful manner. Failure to achieve generativity results in a state of rudderless stagnation. Difficulties in this stage lead to the mid life crisis, a period of intense emotional turmoil due to perceived and real failures in one's life.

As a country, we must define our identity by doing a reality check of who we are and where we are. Taking current inventory of our status. Our national boundaries are fictitious, baseless and founded on not-so-well thought reasons. No more than land demarcations which bear no unique identity? The European powers demarcated our national boundaries as private protectorates for their economic gains, policies controls, cultural expansions and as a show of might among other variables. However, any foreigner visiting our country may notice some of Kenyans unique identities such as: *ugali*, *nyama choma*, noisy and speedy *matatus*, traffic overlapping and our generosity and hospitality especially towards guests. At least we have minimized pick pocketing.

In The Nature and Logic of Capitalism, Robert Heilbroner describes ideologies as "systems of thought and believe by which dominant classes explain to themselves how their social system operates and what principles it exemplifies". In the context of the nation, ideology attempts to give all citizens something to hold in common—an ideal, a past, or a dream for the future. The ideology of the nation is useful in building solidarity among individuals with a common background. However, this solidarity necessarily comes at the cost of excluding those who do not fit this privileged identity.

The nation is ideologically defined as the history held in common between many individuals. Ernest Renan's article "What is a Nation?" discards many possible definitions of the nation. He demonstrates that historical, anthropological, and geographic truths do not support the idea of the nation as defined by a set of geographic borders, shared race or ethnicity, or a common language. Instead, Renan defines the nation as "a large-scale solidarity, constituted by the feeling of the sacrifices that one has made in the past and of those that one is prepared to make in the future" This vision of the nation is evidenced by numerous examples, including the United States' anthem "America." The song identifies America with a shared sacrifice by characterizing the nation as the "land where my fathers died," a reference originally to the Revolutionary War.

France's "Marseillaise" also recalls a revolutionary struggle. The song both calls the citizenry "aux armes (to arms)" against "rois conjures (conspiratorial kings)" and, as Esteban Buch writes in Beethoven's Ninth: A Political History, functionally replaces the aristocracy's elitist "Te Deum" with a French song that common citizens can understand and an elitist choral setting with a simple tune that "eliminates the barrier between musicians and non-musicians and establishes the united voice of the people". This remembrance of national struggle in song creates the nation's identity for the future.

Renan not only contends that national ideology is founded on historical sacrifice - he justifies this ideology. Arguably, a national identity founded on history is as artificial as claiming the political significance of geographic borders. Instead of reflecting history accurately, ideology often constructs a "cult of past heroes". Thus, the nation fails to remember that the Revolutionary War most served to benefit the wealthy merchant class, the United States committed genocide against American native tribes, and Thomas Jefferson owned slaves. However, even if a nation's ideological interpretation of history may be incomplete, Renan argues that citizens have a legitimate duty to and connection with the nation's past: Man does not improvise. The nation, like the individual, is the culmination of a long past of endeavors, sacrifice, and devotion.

33

Renan argues that of all cults, that of the ancestors is the most legitimate, for the ancestors have made us what we are. He believes that because any contemporary nation stands on the shoulders of past giants, it has a duty to give them credit. The ideology of the nation empowers the nation to overcome crises by building unity. Artifacts of national ideology, such as national anthems, loyalty oaths, and invocations of patriotism unite the nation by reminding individuals of the history they share in common with their fellow citizens. For example, the Marseillaise strengthens post-revolutionary France by calling on the present generation to share its ancestors' struggles.

Since the colonial powers ignored communities' identities, some communities like the Somali were harshly separated between Kenya and the Somali republic. The Maasais were divided between Kenyan and Tanzania. Many other community members were equally separated from their extended families. What then would give Kenya a national identity? Or Tanzania, or France or the Comoros or any other nation? Language? Really? Are the county boundaries as ruthless as the European drawn national boundaries? For instance, what unifies the constituents of the Kiambu county – bearing in mind we have Kenyans from all walks of life in this county especially working in the flower farms, coffee and tea estates and the Industrial town of Thika? So many other counties have similar fate. What will give each county a unique identity? And is it necessary in the first place?

From Article 89 of our constitution, constituencies are defined by population quota, geographical features and urban centers, community interest, historical, economic and cultural ties; and means of communication. The defunct IIBRC, by and large, reviewed constituencies with due consideration to the country's scrapped eight provinces and understandably so. The adoption of

34

the IIBRC report by parliament saved the face of IEBC *ab initio* ahead of the all important 2012 first elections under this new constitutional dispensation. Hopefully, merit will override the knack for political pacts in constituting the IEBC unlike what we have witnessed in the recent past. Counties on the other hand are formed by a number of constituencies.

What will give any single county a unique identity devoid of discriminations, prejudices and bigotry? Tribe? Who will protect the endangered language groups together with their culture and traditional values within the counties? As at 1992, Yaaku (Central), Kore (Lamu Island) and Lorkoti, Kinare, Elmolo and Sogoo also called Ogiek people groups in the Rift Valley were extinct. Dahalo, Omotik, Ongamo, Bong'om and Boni are endangered while Burji in the north and Suba at the Kenya-Tanzania border are vulnerable languages. Will they survive in the newly established devolved governance units – counties – under the greed of the big-tribe politics? Where does the identity of the minorities lie?

Structural peace can only be realized when the rights of the minorities are upheld against the monopoly of the majorities. Ways ought to be explored to respect and safeguard the interest of all Kenyans equally to the extent that development within counties must respect the minority groupings. As such, county governments must define higher ideals that all constituents identify with. Leadership must realize that peace is not the absence of war. Even the most naïve in the society as Paulo Freire argues, will protest at prolonged injustice, unfairness and tyrannical leadership as witnessed in the on-going Arab uprising. People power can never be ignored any more, not even the considered minorities. Lasting peace in this globe will only be realized when opportunities are shared equitably among all men.

What gives us identity as a human race? The United States was formed by people from all over Europe and West Africa besides the native Red Indians. Nothing different from the Kenyan situation. The Bantu groups are arguably from the Congo basin, the Nilotic speaking groups from north of Kenya, perhaps today's Sudan and the Cushitic groups from the horn of Africa. In addition we have Kenyan Indians, Arabs and Whites; majority of the latter having their roots from Great Britain. All these people today call themselves Kenyans and rightfully so. As an educated civilized nation, we now have our identity broadened beyond the dictates of tribal lines, color pigmentation and language. Indeed, we have symbols of our unique national identity like our national anthem, national language and flag. County governments will do this country a great favor by unifying members of their counties through our national symbols of unity and purpose; else we will disintegrate incredibly along county boundaries as was witnessed during the civil war in the U.S. in the 1960s.

We as a people are homo-empathic-us. We relate with each other from am empathy point of view. To empathize means to put yourself in somebody else's shoes. To empathize is to civilize. To empathize is to be human. As an individual you cannot be human without the human race. From a psychological point of view, we are daily affected and shaped by the thought systems and lifestyles of those around us. If someone nearby is in pain, grief and great distress, this school of thought suggests that you will share in her sufferings, agonies and frustrations as well. This is nature's norm. Thus, failure to empathize is not natural but an acquired behavioral vice. Killings, murder, robbery, theft, tribalism, nepotism, racism are all acquired behaviors based and directed by background orientations and not our genetic make.

In this new constitutional dispensation, we must all wake up to the call of county and national duty. We must recognize that the government is neither the problem nor the solution. As Bill Clinton once argued, our wrongs must be solved by our rights. We should never again keep our shuttered windows and doors tightly closed when our neighbor is being butchered by robbers. We commend the whole idea of community policing introduced not so long ago. The benefits of this ideology can best be reaped at the county level where people are more cohesive and integrated on more commonly knit identities. With this spirit and attitude, we can defeat the forces of illicit drugs, proliferation of small arms and crime off our streets. With one county identity, we can overcome the selfishness of the past and the individualism mentality that engulfs us in a cocoon of mediocrity and self righteousness.

Some of us in Kenya were oriented as Christians and thus identify with Christians and empathize with the Christian course. Similarly, some Kenyans were oriented as Muslims and thus identify with Islam and consequently empathize and expand the Islam course. True for Hinduism, Buddhism, Sikhism, Judaism, African Tradition Religions and all religious systems. Other social groupings empathize and find consolation amongst Homosexuals, Freemasons, Lotterians, the poor, the political class, the judges, people living with disabilities and all walks of life. Unfortunately, the society is so stereotypic that many individuals hardly accommodate constituents with varying convictions, faiths, persuasions and world view. Many of us tend to believe in the existence of one reality and suppress or exterminate all other realities around us.

In the real sense we are all one. The human race has much more that unites us than what divides us. Classic example is the tragedy that occurred in Haiti recently. Friends and family members were the first respondents to the victims of the earthquake. The government of Haiti followed in the rescue mission. Eventually the neighboring countries like the U.S stood up to be counted among the family of nations in the spirit of good neighborhood. Finally, the entire world marched forward and donations streamed from virtually all corners of the world as many countries identified with Haitians – the human brotherhood, our human identity. The response to the human disaster by the world that had hard hit Haiti demonstrates our human identity.

The billion dollar question that ragingly lingers in my mind is how did the Rwandese within the same national boundaries slaughter each other? How did we maim, rape, kill and displace thousands in the disputed presidential electoral violence of 2007/8? What has a *stolen* election to do with innocent families living in the Rift Valley? Are they the ones who *stole* the election? Why would the world find it easier to identify with, say Haitians, than the residents of Rift Valley would identify with each other? For lasting peace to be within the door steps of reality, we must acknowledge our human identity first. With this paradigm shift in our mind set, we will coexist in harmony with any neighbor across our orphan globe.

There is a particular wasp which lays its eggs on caterpillars. For the eggs to incubate and hatch, they gradually consume the caterpillar to death. Howbeit, this is the only way for the Wasps to survive. Once I asked an anthropologist whether the wasps must lay their eggs on the caterpillar or can't they lay their eggs elsewhere and save the life of the caterpillar. You can imagine my ignorance and shock on this subject as he responded with a resounding `No'. They must lay their eggs on the caterpillar. This is extreme parasitism. Interestingly enough, there are many people who believe that their success is pegged on somebody's failure. That means for them to shine politically, they must destroy the political career of someone else. For them to become rich, someone else must get poorer!

Over the time, I have wondered why Africa is less developed than other continents. As a people, we can have countless excuses from our colonial heritage to the multi-tribal compositions to being late comers in the industrial revolution. Africa as a continent is endowed with many natural resources and many Asian countries got their independence more or less the same time as many African countries. After all some countries like Ethiopia, Liberia and Sierra Leone were never colonized. But how developed are these countries? Identity crisis whose consequence is lack of loyalty helps explain this trend in Africa. Several youths of Arab origin have been used as suicidal bombers. Though this is an unfortunate loyalty, it sends a clear message to the world that Muslim-Arabs have a strong identity.

The answer to the un-development in Africa was explained to me very eloquently by a local industrialist. He told me of a story of a University Professor who studied some lunatics intently from a balcony of a home for the Lunatics. He was amazed that six unarmed guards were in charge of the home of a thousand mad men. He watched the guards closely as they freely walked and interacted with the Lunatics. Finally, he rose from his research desk and sternly warned them that they were on a very dangerous trend. `If a thousand Lunatics united against you six guards, none of you would survive', he argued. The guards laughed at him hysterically and replied, `Professor, for the first time you are dead wrong, mad men can never unite.'

Nothing describes the African curse any more. Mad men can never unite. They fight, acquire and maintain power by force. In West Europe and North America, the business concept is corporate. With growth, company directors invite public shareholding. In the Scandinavian countries, they embrace the cooperatives concept. In Kenya, the founders of estates will rather die than share the cake. At the meantime, they ran out of ideas and their empire begins to crumble. Simply because they cannot welcome others in their so called `hard-earned-money'. Madness. It's not a surprise to find an old man about to rest in peace and he cannot peacefully divide the spoils amongst the children from his own blossom. Then since the kids are equally mad, they cannot share the estate amicably and thus are left slaughtering each other.

At some point, I was appointed the Executive Officer of ADHEK – Association of Developing Horticultural Exporters of Kenya. The members were primarily small and medium scale exporters of horticultural fresh produce who perceived FPEAK (Fresh Produce Export Association of Kenya) as an association for the big boys and thus formed an outfit they could easily identify with. The major objectives for the formation and existence of ADHEK were lobbying for better policies in the industry, compliance with industrial requirements and global standards and market intelligence. The argument behind this was that it was more economical to trade and one umbrella including elimination or minimization of theft from unscrupulous clients overseas.

The ADHEK idea was further extended such that member companies would consolidate their cargo and charter freight thus enjoying economies of scale and minimize freight off loads during the high seasons. The mad Africans we are, exporters began to undercut each other after we made produce pricing available to all members whose intention was to help the exporters to play a lead role in pricing of locally grown commodities. Pricing has been dictated predominantly by the market forces for donkey years. Logical as the idea sounded, it collapsed and aborted not only the dreams of the exporters but the entire supply chain they supported right from the small holder growers to suppliers, transporters and players in the service industries just because we have never learnt how to unite.

At the meantime, none of the importers in Rungis fruits and vegetables market in Paris will allow any exporter from Kenya to supply to another importer from the same market without the consent from the other. They beat us nine – zero, because of their oneness and thus keep dictating the market prices and some of them screwing us since we do not have a common voice. I have been a delegate in the EU-EAC trade negotiations and it always amazes me how the European Union team stands strongly together defending their mean conditionalities. On the contrary, the EAC team contests views and contradicts one another leaving the EU team carrying the day. Last year in particular at the Speke Resort, Kampala, my point that the EU market cannot have it both ways – determine the pricing of commodities whether they are importing or exporting – was speedily short down by fellow EAC members.

Perhaps the EAC has never defined its common identity forthright or our selfish nature as Africans dilly dally the all important unification process. A county too ought to have its own identity – positive identity. Negative identity is characterized by fear. Fear of other tribes. Fear that if a national leader – say, a President – does not come from our county; then we will be forgotten and never succeed. We will never have our turn to *eat*. But worse still is when a county leadership does not see its constituents as members of one family with one identity. During the formation of the respective county governments, the author suggests that the leadership should have clear values they wish to be identified with. Guiding principles for which they are ready to live for and prepared to sacrifice for.

Counties ought to develop clear identities based on competitive advantage over other counties and make maximum use of their comparative edge. The county identities in Kenya should not be based on tribes, race, religion or places of origin. This will be retrogressive in our time and age. It is true that the constitution upholds our native cultures, languages and essential practices. This however should not be misconstrued to imply that counties should be formed on the basis of the language used by the majority in that county. I look forward to the day Hon Otieno Kanjwang (Minister – Immigration) will vie in a county in the former Central Province and Hon Paul Muite (former M.P. Kikuyu) will vie in a county in the former Nyanza province with resounding victory. President Obama won the seat of Chicago Illinois Senate though he was born in Hawaii and a better part of his childhood raised up in Indonesia.

It will be quite interesting to see Hon Gedion Moi (Fomer M.P. Baringo Central) vie in former North Eastern and Hon Charity Ngilu vie in former Western province and win overwhelmingly. James Atebe, born and bled in Kenya was re-elected mayor of mission in the province of British Columbia in Western Canada for a second time in 2008 with an eighty per cent margin. If however a Canadian seeks for elective post in Kenya, my bet is that many leaders will decry loss of sovereignty. Seems like the global village concept is undeniable at this time and age in all walks of life. It will be in the interest of county development to accommodate all Kenyans in any local position of leadership. In so doing, we tap from our diversities, skills, experiences and knowledge that could have been in deficit if restricted within the county boundaries.

Where should a county derive its identity from? Values. Principles. county leaders of necessity must invest in the counties they present. The idea of politicians vying and relocating to rest in the serene Nairobi environs make leaders careless in sincerely safeguarding the constituency they present. Why because they haven't invested reasonably at home. They have nothing to lose if the constituents decide to burn the constituency. The Lord Jesus Christ taught that where the treasures of a man are, there his heart is also. Leadership ought to invest at their home turf to have the feel when their interests are at stake. Perhaps, the constituents should demand their leaders to educate their children within the county they present, be hospitalized there and drink water from the home cisterns. Then they will have a feel and empathize with their constituents from a point of knowledge.

What possible difference would it make if our Prime Minister's Office, H.E. Hon Raila Odinga's house was in Kibera where most Langata constituents live rather than in Karen? What about if President H.E. Hon Mwai Kibaki was treated in a heath center in Othaya after the bad accident he experienced in the 2002 political campaigns? Would relocating our Vice President's base to Mwingi North from Karen improve the livelihoods of the constituents over there? May be it should be demanded that all governors reside in their respective constituencies. And at least a quarter of the working days of the Senators and members of the National Assembly should be spent where they were elected. This might contribute to identifying with the constituents and perhaps aid real development.

Success starts with owning and believing in the county vision. Identifying with the plight on the ground. Having the feel of the suffering millions. Lacking clean water in the house of a leader to passionately lobby for the same in the County Assemblies. Having his/her car stuck during rain falls in the impassable roads. Investing in agriculture and the crops cannot find their way to the market due to poor road networks. Children of leaders attending the local dilapidated schools and health centers. Then and only then can leadership identify with the people. We ought to take leadership to the people now and the leadership should be an exact mirror of the people it presents. The county leadership, both at the legislative and the executive levels should reflect the county identity in their moral values, belief systems, standards of living, educational levels, degrees of tolerance, wisdom and emotional intelligence.

Every county is endowed with enormous resources. None should cry foul. Losers complain on what they do not have. Winners do not concentrate on what they do not have but rather on what they do have. County governments are well advised to maximally utilize human, capital and natural resources endowed within them to uplift the livelihoods of their constituents. As members of a given county get involved in particular economic or sporting activities, they begin to identify with each other. Eventually, they create a unique county identity admired by other counties. With a county identity, constituents will defend their county course against deceit, corruption and retrogressive leadership that takes us back to poverty, disease and illiteracy as we enrich the minority ruling class.

To cope with a changing world, an entity must develop the capacity of shifting and changing - of developing new skills and attitudes; in short, the capability of learning - A De Gues, The Living Company

Lessons From Our History

Never before have Kenyans being more optimistic than shortly after peacefully sending away KANU home following the 2002 elections. We were rated leading in optimism globally. Assurances from our democratically elected leaders were quite wooing. President Kibaki's inaugural speech in a sweepingly crowded uhuru park's most remembered words were: "Zero tolerance to corruption". Indeed Hon Kiraitu Murungi dared former President Moi to go to his rural home in Kabarak and see how a government is run. How much more assurance did the ordinary Kenyan need on the government's commitment to

46

delivery of service? And surely, a surgical cleansing operation began in the Judiciary.

In less than a year, those hopes and dreams were shattered. Dr Chris Murungaru and his cronies remembered all the debts they had accrued during the political campaigns and opportunities they missed to *eat* in Moi's 24 years rein. They vividly recalled Mzee Kenyatta's song.... "My bird *eat* `wisely' for if you are caught, I will not be with you". No one has narrated this corruption attitude more articulately than Michela Wrong in her book, "It's our turn to eat". An attempt by former PS in governance and ethics, John Githongo to reverse the rotting situation put the anti-graft Czar's life on the line leading to his self imposed exile in Britain. Finally, there was negligible difference with President Moi's regime save change of guards. Why then change for change's sake? NARC's pre-election pledges were thwarted due to lack of boldness and decisiveness with the executive to renounce corrupt cronies. Such history is bound to recur unless we put in place decisive and bold leadership at both levels of government.

An almost equivalent laudable spirit of nationalism hovered in the same uhuru park grounds with the promulgation of the new constitution and I fear if the new hope is lost whether it will ever be regained on this side of the great divide for the living generation of Kenyans. By burying our history beneath the carpet, we are bound to repeat it in perfected format and degrees. Yes, at any given moment, we must look forward. But at the same time however, we must draw clear lessons from our history for devolution of governance on its own is a means and not an end to equitable distribution of resources. The residents of Zanzibar coexist peacefully because it is ingrained at infancy. In this tiny island, kids are sternly warned against mistreating visitors, theft and all sorts of crime. You can walk in the dark and congested streets of Zanzibar at any hour. We too need to deeply cultivate another sense of nationhood at the very birth of the county governments.

As I follow the debate surrounding the volatile Hague subject, I am mesmerized by our forgetfulness gifting. The 2007/08 mayhem happened barely three years ago at the writing of this book and interestingly enough the blood of the victims of the violence is still crying for justice. Indeed Ghosts must have killed, raped, maimed, looted and displaced thousands as none of the humans in Kenya is ready to take responsibility. As usual, implicated leaders have devised cunning bravado and braggadocio surrounding their ICC mentioning and taken quick refuge behind tribal cocoons with ethnic jingoism. This is not new in Kenya. Of late, many African countries bracing for elections have been warned not to go the Kenyan way. Even in Zimbabwe, Robert Mugabe sternly warned against the Kenyan-style electoral viles. And surely enough, it did not happen. So, is there any lesson that we ought to learn never to stoop this low again?

Time and again it has been said that those who forget history are condemned to repeat it. Oft times historical events have parallels in the present. The Uhuru park blasts on June 13 this year have a parallel with the grisly murder of J.M. Kariuki in 1975. Prior to his killing, innocent Kenyans were killed in a bomb blast at the OTC bus station. At the meantime, then vice president, Daniel Moi deceived the nation that J.M. was in a trip in Zambia. At the height of the 2007/8 ethinic violence, a specific ethnic community had 23 members burnt alive in a Kiambaa K.A.G church. This has a parallel in the Rwandese massacre and the extermination by Adolf Hitler of very specific groupings in their hamlets and synagogues: Jews, Catholics, Homosexuals and Gypsies. Hitler called it the Aryan cleansing. Isn't this similar to the ongoing expulsion of the Roma (Gypsies) by the French? Isn't this happening at the watch of the Human Rights activists from the West?

How kind is history's judgment to Adolf Hitler of Germany, Pol Pot of Cambodia, Slobodan Milosevic of Yugoslavia, Augostino Pinochet of Chile, Idi Amin of Uganda and Radovan Karadzic who is now being tried at The Hague for deaths after the Siege of Sarajevo and the Srebrenica Massacre during the Bosnian War in 1995. Someone keep a watch against historical tyrannies. The current Arab uprisings have their parallels with the quest for independence of the 50s and 60s in the last century. In his book, *A Journey*, former British Premier, Tony Blair, says he was 'desperately' sorry over casualties on all sides. Who will stop a future Blair – Bush alliance from invading a sovereign nation in the disguise of weapons of mass destruction, or baptized another name? The guardians of historical lessons are the good people who are tortured by historical ills.

Is the concept of County governments completely new in Kenya? Not at all. The original Lancaster Constitution had a senate composed of 42 representatives from each of the country's administrative districts. It complemented the Lower House in policy making and checking the Executive. However, the original Lancaster Constitution was grossly mutilated through several amendments after independence and finally the Senate was dissolved in 1966 and replaced with a National Assembly on the grounds of cutting government expenses. What, good people, will bar a historical repeat of similar magnanimity? Do we only hope that such will never recur or will we take responsibility as the custodians and guardians of this new governance dispensation?

The ghost of historical injustices has strangled us since the declaration of independence. Lives have been lost, thousands displaced and voices of reason silenced. Great human rights activists like the Rev Dr. Timothy Njoya bitterly humiliated and tortured at full camera scenes. One victim of Nyayo house, Wallace Gichere, a journalist was crippled in both legs when police threw him out of the window of his third floor apartment. Writers like Ngugi Wa Thiongo went into political exile. Leaders like Paul Muite, Kiraitu Murungi and Dr Gibson Kamau Kuria had to go hiding locally or were whisked away in secret to safer havens abroad.

Ahead of the original Saba Saba Day on July 7, 1990, Dr. Gibson Kuria was spirited out of the country by the U.S embassy to avoid the Moi regime crack down – arrests and detentions without trial. Kenneth Matiba, Charles Rubia, Raila Odinga, Gitobu Imanyara and Mohammed Ibrahim were arrested and detained without trial. When Dr John Khaminwa duly went to press for the release of these veterans, he `vanished' within the bowels of the police station.

The manner in which people were treated was brutally primitive. Leaders like Charles Rubia and Rev. Dr. Timothy Njoya were frog-marched into police vehicles. By the time Kenneth Matiba left Kamiti Maximum security prison, his body was frail as his heath began to deteriorate. At the writing of this book, he walks with a shuffled limp. The post colonial leadership in Kenya was oppressive to say the least until the exit of the KANU government. Being expelled from KANU spelt the death-knell for any political career and businesses squashed for the prominent that were in the opposition league.

In his 1967 book, *A Grain of Wheat*, Ngugi Wa Thiong'o, painted a vivid picture of the frantic preparations and the nervous anticipation on the eve of the 1963 celebrations. Ngugi's warning about the follies of mistaken heroism was prophetic. Hardly had the Independence dust settled than the leadership of the country rewarded sly but undeserving lackeys and sidelining the individuals who bore the real sacrifice. I have no earthly idea whether the heroes of the so called 'Second Republic' have been recognized by the current coalition regime. However I know that all cabinet ministers serving in the current government have been accorded, as is the tradition, the Elder of the Golden Heart honour – never mind the criteria behind the recognition.

A commission was established under the watch of one, Bethuel Kiplagat, in the name of The Truth Justice and Reconciliation Commission. The Truth Justice and Reconciliation Act says in Sections 5(1)(a) that the Commission must establish "an accurate, complete and historical record of violations and abuses of human rights and economic rights inflicted on persons by the state, public institutions and holders of public office both serving and retired." Bethuel Kiplagat has been recognized by the current government as a peace maker. But who is this man Bethuel Kiplagat? Is this a repeat of our history of awarding losers and damping the real defenders of peace? What achievements have Julius Sunkuri made to be appointed the Kenyan lead diplomat in China?

The good intent of the Truth Justice and Reconciliation Commission is well understood by all. The question that hovered in the minds of many Kenyans however was whether Bethuel Kiplagat had the necessary goodwill from Kenyans to steer this vehicle forward. Can we honestly separate the message from the messenger? Can the northern Kenyan families that were torturously humiliated and others lost lives during the Wagalla massacre when Ambassador Kiplagat was the P.S in charge of security accommodate his reconciliatory efforts? Whether he played a role or not is a different matter altogether. Of importance here is that he has been implicated, period. This argument is based on the mere fact that we have hundreds of women and men in Kenya who have not been implicated at all and have the capacity to give

51

TJRC the commensurate leadership it calls for and deserves. Why must our current governing authorities only feel secure with the old guard even when retaining the old wineskin jeopardizes the promised dream of breaking from the past grafts, felonies, assassinations, tribalism, crime, diseases and poverty among countless national woes?

Is this commission meant to appease the 'Big Brother' of the West or was it instituted for the country's good? May be he is a very experienced diplomat. Experienced? Why then didn't we hire the Samuel Kivuitu team to head the IIEC in conducting the historic referendum? I congratulate Betty Kaari Murungi, the former TJRC's vice chair for quitting after trying so hard to salvage the already delicate 'peace search' engine. Had the other commissioners followed in her worthy footsteps, perhaps Diplomat Kiplagat would have thought twice. Kiplagat's name has been adversely linked with the Ndung'u land report, the Robert Ouko case and in the Wagalla massacre. His purported public service cannot and should not be separated from public perception. There is no way under heaven we can wish our history to just rest in peace.

The disbanded Electoral Commission of Kenya failed the state miserably especially when its leader, Samuel Kivuitu, acknowledged ignorance of the presidential candidate that won the 2007 general elections. That ECK team is partly to blame for the blood bath and displaced families. Certainly, they created loopholes for rigging elections either directly or by doing nothing to seal rigging possibilities. In contrast Issack Hassan, though inexperienced in electoral processes led the Interim Independent electoral commission that conducted the 2010 referendum professionally, ethically and with an unquestionable sense of responsibility. ECK and IIEC had similar mandate to a large extent but one was led by tired bed fellows while one was led by a new brand of results-driven professionals. Nothing wrong with age in years but everything wrong with old corrupt practices and habits.

Our history teaches with unmistakable emphasis that you cannot separate the system from the actors. Hardly can you teach an old dog new tricks. Again this shouldn't be misconstrued to imply age in numbers as some perpetuate this propaganda but rather age in retrogressive character devoid of new workable ideas. Character formation is a life-long process. It is not a destination but a journey. We cannot entrust the new constitutional order to non reformers and anticipate positive change just because we now have the institutional framework. We must go beyond the incredible institutions that the new order has instituted and deliberately but genuinely subject all trustees of public officers to severe public scrutiny.

For instance, with all due respect to the outgoing and long serving Attorney General, Amos Wako, our history clearly demonstrates his incapability or unwillingness to execute justice to the culprits of graft, extra judicial killings, ethnically instigated violence and electoral malpractices. How then in the name of common sense can we entrust him to mid wife the implementation of the new constitution? Has he ever been a legal reformer? Do we want to bury our heads in the sand like the legendary ostrich and appoint him in a different high flying national position in the name of experience? My sixth sense tells me that he is highly likely to run for a public office and interestingly enough Kenyans will vote him in since he has the bucks. What a tragedy to democracy and vivid demonstration of our historical ignorance?

In February 2009, Prof Phillip Alston, the U.N Special Rapporteur on extra judicial executions described Amos Wako most vividly:

"He is the chief obstacle to prosecuting anyone in authority for extra judicial killings. He has presided for a great many years over a system that is clearly bankrupt in relation to dealing with police killings and has done nothing to ensure that the system is reformed. Public statements lamenting the system's shortcomings have been utterly unsupported by any real action. In brief, Mr Wako is the embodiment in Kenya of the phenomenon of impunity. The resignation of the Attorney General is an essential first step to restoring the integrity of the office and ending its role in promoting impunity in Kenya."

Despite possessing the most impeccable academic credentials, Amos Wako was Kenya's Attorney General during the tribal clashes of 1992-3, 1997 and 2007-8. No main suspect has he prosecuted since. He has either denied or frustrated justice for those who suffered in the Nyayo house chambers. He either hands in inadequate and late reports on human rights abuse or never at all tarnishing our national image as abusers of human rights. He has never concluded gross cases of graft like Goldenberg and Aglo leasing. He could have borrowed a leaf from former Attorney General Charles Njonjo – the black British – who watched significant constitutional damages take place. Whenever injustice will be recorded in the annals of our history, a harsh opinion must also be held against Justice Mathew Guy Muli who used his constitutional powers to help the then Executive in the suppression of dissent.

Whereas the author would have preferred to avoid mentioning names that would easily be interpreted as character assassination by skeptics, lessons from our history would have remained ambiguous. Specific examples on how justice has been slaughtered under merciless watchers is meant to emphasis the message that welcoming the new constitution is a bridge rather than an end. History repeats itself. If we entrust this momentous document to irresponsible leadership, chances are that clauses can be repealed to suit interests. Well intended clauses will be sacrificed in the pursuit of fame and fortune. We must never go back. We must never forget our history and thus expose ourselves to wolfish criminals under the disguise of leaders.

In seeking future lasting justice, the buck must stop somewhere. Someone must take responsibility. No one understood this more clearly that the 33rd U.S. President, Harry Truman who reputedly reorganized government structures perhaps than any other President. He famously pronounced on his desk, "The buck stops here." Hubert Humphrey said unless there is justice for all, there is justice for none. John F Kennedy believed that freedom is indivisible; when one man is free, all are; when one is enslaved, all are. Our history must earnestly equip us to demand the buck to stop somewhere and annihilate grey lines of responsibilities. By his resignation, President Richard Nixon put the interest of his country above personal vindication. I am yet to understand why it takes so much public and political pressure for our leaders to give in even when they are clearly in the wrong.

From a global perspective, leaders have betrayed followers in the last century. Around six million German Jews suffered in the evil hands of Nazi leader, Adolf Hitler. Over ten million Russians were slain by their leader Joseph Stalin. Close to fifteen million Chinese farmers were exterminated by their leader Mao Tse Tung. Thousands of Iraq citizens were brutally killed by Saddam Hussein and so were Ugandans under the strong man, Idi Amin Dada. The list is endless. To counter such future possibilities in our world, history must be reviewed and bottle necks sorted not only institutionally but also by fixing men and women of good will and proven character to foster reforms. This message was no timelier than in the formation of the county governments in Kenya's second republic.

Even at such an early age in the world's quest for democracy way back in 1776, George Washington, helped the United States to act in the country's good will by handing over power peacefully after serving two terms in office. This was despite his grueling sacrifice for his country in their war for independence from the British Empire. For us to break from our past injustices, we ought to be vigilant in scrutinizing those we entrust with the vital documents and reform positions. Our history will record August the 4th 2010 as the day when Kenyans spoke up unequivocally to change every aspect of our governing institutions. We must not rest on the laurels. We face now as a country one of our most dramatic times and we cannot relax our vigilance in enhancing a smooth transition to a new era of prosperity, faith and harmonious co-existence characterized by servitude leadership.

Good leadership is not necessarily brandished by intellect nor does it possess the most alluring visage, but women and men who through selfless determination, ingenuity and wise counsel help the populace achieve its goals. It is Lenin who in 1920 that said as good communists and Leninists, the Soviet Union's repudiate all morality that comes outside of class walls or originates from some supernatural ideas. All morality must proceed from class concepts and be used for unifying the proletariat. Genius as he was, Lenin ignored all aspects of Godly morality and propagated intellectualism solely in the leadership of the Soviet Union. No wonder that empire crumbled and their heightened pride humbled. We are not just logical people but we are emotional people as well. People don't care how much leaders know, but how much they care.

A historical concern that cannot be overlooked at this juncture has to do with the land question in Kenya. Issues rotating around this subject have political, economic and legal aspects. The political aspects are set in the structure of the colonial administration. The crown of Great Britain was the centre of all power and controlled all resources. Anyone holding land was only doing it on behalf of the crown. The beneficiaries of the best land were, therefore, those closest to the crown. These were mainly settlers, the missionaries, colonial chiefs and collaborators.

The transfer of power from the colonial authorities to indigenous elites did not lead to fundamental restructuring of the land legacy as expected. The crown was merely represented by the President with the land administration infrastructure remaining intact. The President being the centre of political power remained with full control of land ownership, distribution and management. This has been manifested in gross disparities in land ownership, general deterioration in productivity, severe land pressure, speculative hoarding, landlessness and squatter problems, destruction of forests and wetlands, discrimination in land administration, public land-grab, lengthy land cases, gender discrimination, food insecurity and poverty.

For food security, equity distribution of resources, increased productivity, enhanced livelihoods, preservation of our wetlands and forest cover to be achieved, the county governments must pursue the spirit of the current land policy as outlined in the new constitution. Failure to learn lessons from our history risks sinking in the same quagmire of defeatism. It is my concerted effort to persuade the Kenyan citizenry to draw clear lessons from our history for the purposes of avoiding the pitfalls while forming the county governments. We have a noble chance to start up clean, maintain freedom like the Americans proudly call their country; the land of the free. We must enhance the equality of all men, respect human rights and put leadership in place that truly reflects the image and will of the electorate.

Kenya's body politic on close examination of her history shows a confounding ambivalence to the direction that the nation desires to take on an array of issues, notably graft and impunity. Our woes will neither be the absence of good laws nor runaway graft in this new constitutional dispensation. Rather it will be our indifference to blatant corruption and baseless protection of those grossly indicted in graft and impunity which reveals a deeply ingrained flawed societal character. An enormous amount of introspection and deliberate overhaul of these collective flaws must be taken for us to realize the change advanced in the new constitutional order.

It is unbelievable the extent to which controversies surrounding the corruption monster segue so seamlessly into political careers even among first time legislators. Albeit the commoner in Kenya is rarely considered a paragon of efficiency in our national discourse, there is the occasional superb performer who lends the service a modicum of accountability, though a minute percentage. This individual public servant is nothing but a laughing stock amongst colleagues who wonder why he cannot garner himself a fortune with the public coffers. This is the individual we must creatively seek to award to maintain the momentum we have gained in our quest for better governance.

I never contemplated in my wildest imaginations that an endorsement by Mungiki would one day be a treasure pot for Nairobi seats. Undoubtedly, this legitimizes the prescribed sect and tantamount accords it a firm clout. No wonder crooks with murky pasts find their way to our house of honor and are celebrated as heroes and never treated as villains! We should disengage prospective leaders' populism from their criminality. That is why those behind the killings of Fr. John Kaisser, Robert Ouko and Bishop Alexander Mugo must be brought to book through our new judicial order. Otherwise, the new constitutional order will turn out to be another mirage.

As Koigi Wamwere once noted, though the first nationalists spent many years fighting for change from colonialism to independence, when the trophy came, it was given, not to them, but to people who had fought against *uhuru* – home guards and their educated children. Again, though it was the second liberators who sacrificed to change Kenya from one-party dictatorship to multiparty democracy, the trophy went, not to the badly-injured wrestlers with the dragon of tyranny, but to perpetrators of dictatorship and their children. After ignoring history, for a third time, we are betraying change by giving the trophy of the new constitution, not to those who fought longest and hardest for the dream of democracy, but to fence-sitters, anti-reformers, latter-day democrats, and the scions of aristocracy, whose objective is to entrench the *status quo*.

Most of us however watched in disbelief the union between Koigi Wamwere and retired President Moi fighting against the new constitution despite the former's detention by the latter. I thought principles governed Koigi's ideology rather than mere politicking and selfish public attention seeking. This has long characterized Kenya's leadership. Pursuit of personal interests. Once many reformers get into parliamentary elective politics, ideals they once held are sacrificed at the altar of political survival. Dr Sally Kosgei made it plain that she will go it the Hon Ruto (William) way since her political survival is pegged upon her community's goodwill rather than on principles governing the impunity question that has adversely touched her tribal kingpin. All Luo Nyanza legislators dance Hon Raila's tune whether he is in the right or not; and so do most PNU allied MPs sing H.E. Kibaki's music. We have a few exceptions to this trend like the outspoken Hon Gitobu Imanyara and the fire breathing Hon Martha Karua whom we can only hope will find their way back to elective leadership in 2012 for going against the local current.

Real change as envisioned by the *mwananchi* means equitable distribution of resources to all regardless of their family name, tribal background or political affiliation. This kind of change can only happen if those appointed in implementing the new constitution are first committed to the change aspired by Kenyans collectively and have unquestionable history of reformation. Seeking for people experienced in the KANU machinations will only protect the status quo and speedily scatter the hopes and dreams of the commoners in this country who have been sidelined by bureaucracies and monopolies. We the ordinary *wananchi* must aslo break from our past failures by judging leaders on the grounds of their character and ideals rather than on seasonal political waves and regional kingpins dictatorships who mislead the masses for personal gain.

We need a leadership that protects the farmer from the greed of monopoly. A leadership that does not brutally protect the fat cats in the oil industry for self corrupt gains and one who gets sleepless nights at the memory of the IDPs' plight. Kate Halff, the head of the Internal Displacement Monitoring Center, a Geneva-based project of the Norwegian Refugee Council and Michel Gabaudon, President of Refugees International, an independent Washington DC based organization that advocates ending refugee crisis, argues that more than 40% of all IDPs are in Africa. Seeing the trend as a disgrace to the continent, this pandemic ought to be a wake-up call for all the 53 AU member states.

To address our continental history, AU adopted the Convention for the Protection and Assistance of IDPs in Africa, popularly known as the Kampala Convention on October 23rd, 2009. Since then, it has been signed by 29 members but ratified by two,

Uganda and Sierra Leone. However, to enter into force and become legally binding, the Convention has to be ratified by 15 countries. Ordinary Kenyans would have expected such a bill to be of priority in our legislative assembly. Perhaps, our leaders do not want such commitments lest they find themselves with similar predicament like the signing of the ICC Rome statute. The public ought to rise up for the course of the IDPs relentlessly and keep leadership on reality check.

Justice ought to be re-defined. The American declaration for independence has this to say of justice, "All men are created equal, that they are endowed by their Creator with certain inalienable rights; that among these are life, liberty and pursuit of happiness." Justice for IDPs living in squalor in camps and the millions living in deplorable conditions in Kenya has enemies galore. As Okiya Omtatah Okoiti puts it, to crush old and prevent new corruption, the war must be fought scientifically, impartially and in good faith, acquiring a proactive life and purpose of its own, professionally anchored in the rule of law, and free from political machinations. Only thoroughness and fidelity to due process will determine guilt and stop the war from becoming a political tool of new impunity and corruption by opportunists and wheeler-dealers cashing in on public outrage that is rightly driving the hemorrhage at the top.

This was best seen by the motion moved by one, Dr Boni Dixon Khalwale as he moved the vote of no confidence motion against Finance Minister Amos Kimunya's involvement in the controversial sale of the Grand Regency hotel in July 2008. This led pious emotional debate in parliament but nonetheless, as much as Hon Kimunya was reinstated back to cabinet, the circumstances leading to possible hefty loses of public funds were, to some good extent, clarified. It is this sort of aggression watch dog responsibility from the public, the civil society and legislators of good will that will safeguard economic justice for the majority from the mutating monster of graft. We hope Dr Khalwale, a gifted parliamentary debater will bounce back to the August house following the court ruling against his election in the 2007 flawed elections.

We then must look into the future with clear and deep reflections of our past as we earnestly seek to build indomitable county governments. The good traditions must be upheld while the selfish ones discarded speedily. The selfish lessons of our freedom fighters need to be taught in our schools to pass on the legacy of their heroic struggles. At the same time, future generations must be sternly warned from the ills of yesteryears that have impoverished Africa. Ancient civilizations like Chinese once fell down but patriotic leadership revitalized that great economy and maintaining record growth rate for almost half a century since World War Two. So did Japan. So has Germany after the unification becoming the greatest economy in Europe. We too can do it. Good governance has made one Korea very prosperous while bad governance has made one Korea wallow in abject poverty and madly enough preoccupied with making nuclear weapons that cannot feed its populace.

Our prosperity, by and large, depends on the county leadership we put in place rather than merely the writings in the constitution and the choice is in our hands. The collective success of all counties summates to the national progress. The temptation of underrating the role of the county leadership can be great in respect to the national seats. We must remember at any given moment that the county government is assigned to a great extent the responsibility of reaching down to the detailed needs in the communities from hunger, security, education, water and all social development issues. We thus must see the counties as autonomous subsets of a bigger whole each carrying unique but intertwined roles.

Humbly guarded and safely guided by clear lessons from our history, we can achieve the dream of a better tomorrow for all Kenyans. A quick glimpse into our historical injustices will explain why the independence struggles of poverty, disease and illiteracy still linger around us 48 year later. In the "Pedagogy of the Oppressed", the author, Paulo Freire was perplexed by the fact that so many people "just don't seem to care" about changing or improving their situation. Instead, they just accept their situation as given. Hence, he postulated that people lived at 3 levels of awareness; and that they acted differently at each of these levels.

The first level is "Magic". They explain the events and forces that shape their lives in terms of myths, magic, or powers beyond their understanding and control. They are fatalistic – every-thing is 'God's will': ordained from beyond them. The second level is naïve. This level no longer passively accepts the hardships of being 'on the bottom'. Instead, they try to adapt so as to make the best of the situation in which they find themselves – imitating mannerisms of those at the top. The third level he called critical. These people use scientific process – observation and critical thinking to explain the causes of poverty and other human problems. They question the values, rules and expectations passed down by those in control – whose benefit are these rules.

History supports this theory that even people who are at the "Magic" level of awareness will protest at some point if perpetually oppressed by the oppressor as was witnessed with the Arab uprising of the 2011. For leadership to be sustainable, it must then respect human dignity and seek to make humanity better and all citizens independent.

Leadership is getting others to do what you want them to do because they want to do it - Eisenhower

The County Leadership

Edmund Burke, the mercurial British philosopher and statesman described parliamentary leadership so eloquently in his words: "Parliament is not a congress of ambassadors from different and hostile interests; which interests each must maintain, as agents and advocates; but parliament is a deliberative assembly of one nation with one interest, that of the whole; where not local purposes, not local prejudices ought to guide, but the general good, resulting from the general reason of the whole. You chose a member indeed; but when you have chosen him, he is not a member of Bristol but a member of parliament".

The architects of parliamentary democracy never intended that house to be a fat cow joint but a true representative of the character, aspirations and wishes of the people they present. The day is coming when the electorate will rise up to the occasion and elect a wo/man based purely on merit generated from his qualities, abilities, gifting and character rather than on the pennies s/he can dish during electioneering to the majority desolate populace. When that day finally comes, we shall have true servant-hood leadership characterized by humility and capacity whereby all leaders will work together as a team with no partisan divisive positions while making decisions of national interest. By embracing this attitude in the elections of our county leadership during its sunrise, we shall bring to reality this day.

The brouhaha that surrounded the boundaries demarcated for the 80 newly created constituencies by the Andrew Ligale led team riveted parliament with one plank calling for "population quota" *modus operadi* fairly informed the process while the other stridently averred gerrymandering; I feel like Speaker Kenneth Marende should recite the words of Edmund Burke to our Parliamentarians. This is simply because they appointed the Interim Independent Boundaries Review Commissioners. Did parliamentarians expect IIBRC to be a butt of stooges and quislings like the bootlickers that surrounded the Moi Presidency? Mine here is not to defend the IIBRC but to emphasize the need to unequivocally respect institutions. Vetting of institutional holders should precede their commissioning; otherwise courts will always be scrapped once the mighty and strong are charged amounting to anarchy.

The same behavior was witnessed recently when the Ndaragwa legislator, Jeremiah Kioni accused The Hague of double standards. Certainly, the West practices double standards in many cases regarding international justice. No wonder the U.S. rejects with cynics-tic arrogance to be a signatory to the Rome Statute that forms the ICC with gung ho. Otherwise, many U.S. leaders would spend a life time under the global opprobrium for crimes against humanity committed in Iraq, Afghanistan, Somalis, Chile, Vietnam, DRC, Timor, Columbia, Grenada, Iran, Kosovo, Guatemala, Libya, Laos and Palestine. But U.S. leaders have forethought. Our leaders have afterthought. "Let's not be vague, say Hague", our MPs acclaimed. After their political life lines were offered residence at the The Hague palatial home, "We are a sovereign state; let us withdraw from the Rome Statute".

Our good MPs initially preferred The Hague for the suspects of the 2007/8 post election violence following the botched elections to a local tribunal as proposed by the government particularly by Martha Karua on February 12th 2009 and March 2nd 2009. The cabinet too rejected Mutula Kilonzo's draft bills on a local tribunal on July 14th and 30th 2009 preferring the Hague option. After both the PNU and ODM were adversely affected by the naming of the suspects by Moreno Ocampo, the ICC Chief Prosecutor on Wednesday the 15th 2010; our leaders cried foul. They forgot one should stop digging once she finds herself in a hole as they put it in Westminster. This implies that previous decisions were not based on principles but for political conveniences.

We have had a crop of some political leaders who often than not are pugnacious. The cacophony around the yearned change process masks slow progress on a key factor necessary for the successful transition to the Kenya we want. This is the struggle between competition and cooperation in our politics. We often try to pull each other down rather than to work for the common good. Whereas competitive politics is supposed to help us identify the best minds for leadership, it often gives birth to the leadership characterized by voter buying and higher endorsements by the big-boy parties. This gives rise to a political leadership providing largesse to cohorts of supporters assuring them that their interest will be taken care of. This unhealthy competition if extended to the county levels, will certainly lead to violence between counties and locking out opportunities from members outside a given county especially on tribal identities.

As a nation, we need to put in place county leadership that will encourage brotherhood across different ethnic groups and counties to build a strong national synergy that will propel the national economy forward. No group can survive let alone flourish single handedly. We will succeed by capitalizing on the competitive advantage of each group tapping into the various potentials and peculiar values presented by each county as the only remedy to grow a sustainable and stable nation. Efforts by any county, no matter how endowed with resources, natural and human, will remain sun-optimal if there is no goodwill to knit the strengths of all the other counties in re-building a prosperous Kenya.

The success of organizations, institutions and countries as well is determined by countless factors but the leading among them is leadership. Leadership is the ability to influence behavior. Historically speaking, we have had brilliant academic giants that led their countries to the doldrums and less schooled individuals who led their followers into prosperity. Dr. Robert Mugabe, for instance, led his country from the arms of the colonial powers relatively well between 1980 and 1990 just to wallow later in the excuses of the colonial mishaps in the 90s to the writing of this book. This has *helped* Zimbabwe to record inflation rates never reached since the beginning of times. Never mind that Dr. Mugabe has seven University degrees, all earned!

Perhaps a weak comparative analysis would be Zimbabwe's neighboring country. Presently, the country's President, Jacob Zuma, has no formal education and is steering the country forward including mastering the art of handling a polygamous family! I wouldn't attempt to take after our education system or our educators at all. I really do not think that we have an educational problem, per se, in Kenya, but a societal tragedy. Most of our legislators today are highly educated individuals but only few of them have the requisite commitment needed to move the country forward. We must go beyond one's educational achievements to stability of character, emotional intelligence and personal past records. We cannot afford to accept financial gifting from drug barons and `reformed' gangsters and expect such leadership to instill desired values in our youths. Role modeling from such leadership compromises the moral fabric of our great nation and makes us but a laughing stock amongst the community of nations.

But may be natural resources are the ultimate solution to a nation's economy and not the leadership qualities? Really? The Democratic Republic of Congo is endowed with enormous natural resources. The Congolese must be filthy wealthy individuals? Or, are they? Isn't the story similar for Zambia and its copper belt? The oil rich Southern Sudan. Nigeria and her oil? Zimbabwe's vast mineral reserves including gold? Ironically, Japan has no real natural resources and has been, for long, the largest credit nation in the world. Seems the prosperity of a nation calls for more than educated leadership and endowment with natural resources. It calls for leadership.

Leadership is influence. Good leadership is good influence. As H Jackson Brown Jnr once noted, "Our character is what we do when we think no one is looking". One's leadership style is defined by his character. There are many leadership styles employed for varying reasons and on merit and by different leaders. Most common leadership styles that are assumed are:

- Autocratic Leadership: - Under this style of leadership, the leader is never questioned. S/he is Mrs/Mr know-it-all. Period. It's dictatorial in nature and ignores institutionalized leadership. It's running a government by the leader's intuition. This leads people into worshiping the leader, boot licking and produces sycophants in a nation. It suppresses the voice of reason; it kills innovation and undermines talents, aptitudes, gifting and art. All county constituents MUST enhance an accountable and transparent leadership. The chapter of mere excuses of being misused by the leaders they elected into office must be closed. We must take responsibility for our county's success or failure and stop blaming our geographical location or/and inadequacy of natural resources as well as infrastructures. We must be solution conscious and not problem conscious.

- Collaborative Leadership: - No one truly mastered the art of collaborative leadership than the colonial masters. Indeed our forefathers have passed on the story that the British came with one hand holding the Bible while the other was holding the gun. This argument was used to explain how native sins confessed before priests were known by the ruling class in minute details. The use of home guards was the epitome of collaborative leadership in our colonial history. Our past two regimes used the same leadership approach under the disguise of the Intelligence secret service.

This leadership model breeds mistrust and instills public fear. We, as a people, must refrain from entertaining this approach in our county governance. We are in a new dawn of openness and trust is a non negotiable ingredient to the county's success. Rewarding close confidants to the county leadership using public utilities must be slaughtered in the altar of accountable citizenry before it even sees the light of the day.

- Democratic Leadership: - In this approach to leadership, you let the people decide their fate. As Americans oftenly put it: the World of the free. As such, people are allowed to make free choices. As John F. Kennedy while addressing a crowd in Berlin once said: "Freedom has many difficulties and democracy is not perfect; but we have never had to put a wall; to prevent our people from leaving us". Truly, we have been fighting for democratic space thus the agitation of constitutional reforms. But democracy has given fertile ground to greed, monopoly and corruption all in the name of capitalism. Certainly, the pros of democracy far outweigh the cons; only if the people are in the fore front for their democratic course to yield lasting results.

As one American President said, "The price of democracy is eternal vigilance. And next time they say 'we are asking the government to help us' they will know they are the government."The New law will not be the magic bullet to end greed. Only a vigilant public can stop taxpayers' money finding itself into corrupt officials' big bellies. The county constituents must be part and parcel of the county leadership or else it was pointless to devolve the government in the first place.

- Servant-hood Leadership:- This is the highest level of leadership. In Servant hood leadership, you don't tell people what to do; you lead them in what to do. As the Chinese put it; the world would be clean if everyone swept outside their own house(s).

Leaders tell, good leaders explain, superior leaders demonstrate, great leaders inspire.

Our counties need leaders who understand that it is a call to serve; not to exploit. While electing leaders into public offices, the electorate must now desist from stooping too low as to be bought with pennies at the expense of their prosperity. The back must stop somewhere this time round. It must stop with us, the people of Kenya and not the leadership. We have ways and means of recalling leaders. Should we even get there in the first place rather than having it right from the outset? How then, can we know a servant leader?

Characteristics of Servant Leadership

Former U.S. Presidents Jimmy Carter, Bill Clinton and George W. Bush were governors before they became presidents. They were able to demonstrate to their country women and men that the success they engineered in their respective states could be replicated the country over. This is a leaf worth borrowing. The question that we must now debate is whether our county governors should be leaders or managers. What gifting, talents, skills and aptitudes must county governors, possess?

Managers maintain systems while leaders confront systems. Managers follow set out procedures while leaders direct innovation. My take is that the county leadership calls for leaders who are gifted managers. Leaders who will reach out to people and inspire them to action as well as managers who are keen to plan and remain accountable to the people. Thus the county leadership ought to be run by motivated and people oriented professionals. Professionals who are keen to form accountable and modern systems that embrace art and technological advances and at the same time; men and women who inspire vision. Management of a county, which will be headed by a county governor should only be entrusted with leaders who qualify to head our parastatals like NewKCC, Kenya Airways and many others.

The electorate should be enlightened accordingly to vet leadership alongside this argument. We ought to see county governors as men and women who can be groomed to run for the presidency. The results they produce at the county levels should be their certificate for higher competitive offices. No wonder they can only run the county for only two terms and show case their performance. Senators on the other hand should be men and women who understand county issues and have legislative capacities to present their constituents in parliamentary debates. This then requires a balance of many factors ranging from academia, experience, inspirational skills and more importantly, service.

Characteristics of a servant leader are perhaps as many as the number of writers and trainers on the face of the earth. Nonetheless, a few have been identified by the author as a guideline to provoke the curious minds of the electorate while choosing officials for public offices. Some of the most crucial characteristics that we ought to be on the on-look include:

Strong positive mental work attitude: - Servant leaders must be totally convinced beyond any doubt that the counties they lead will succeed. This success is independent on whether they will be elected or not. Our attitudes determine our altitudes. No journey is too far to walk; no mountain is too high to climb; no task is too difficult to accomplish, it's all in the mind. If a leader does not have faith in ALL the constituents having all necessary basic amenities like education, health, security, food and clean environment; s/he has no business in leading his/her people. One cannot take the people where s/he doesn't believe in the possibilities.

Even at the blink of war, Sir Winston Churchill encouraged the Britons when he said: `Never, never, never give up, conquer we must and conquer we shall'. In 1941 on December 7$^{th}$ when the U.S. was attacked by the Japanese empire, Franklin Delano Roosevelt told the American people: `In my Righteous mind, no matter how long it will take us, the American People will win this war'. Leaders must remain positive in winning the war against poverty, sickness and illiteracy. Winning requires having a clear mental picture of the desired results before which nothing can be accomplished. The county leader must remain positive on his/her picture of the constituency s/he wants to see at the end of her/his term in office.

A leader cannot perform in a manner that is inconsistent with his or her level of association. We must watch out the company that our leaders feel comfortable to hang out with. This depicts his/her true character. A positive leader encompasses around positive individuals and materials; speaks positively and exposes him/herself only to positive information, print or electronic.

74

Very Passionate on their calling: - Servant leaders have an overwhelming desire to succeed. An un-stoppable drive to excel. They must be so consumed with the success of the county that everything else is secondly. They ought not to put their personal interest before the interests of the people they serve. Mother Teresa's passion for the poor Indians in the Calcutta ghetto made her live in seemingly destitute situations. Rosa Park's passion for equal rights made her risk her live during the days of racial segregation in the U.S. Indeed it's her courage that inspired Martin Luther King Junior and consequently an entire people marched forward. We must elect leaders who dream, breath and think of the county's success with every instinct of their being.

We have had Kenyans who were passionate on their professional cause. Carey Francis with his Mathematics class; Dr Griffins with the Education of the poor boy child and George Adamson with the Lions. We have also had countless Kenyans of nativity who are very passionate on their cause. To them I say today, bravos! Let's keep the fire burning for a brighter tomorrow looking forward to the day of prosperity and good will for all Kenyans. Let us never feel drowned in a dungeon that will never lead to a way out but rather see the brilliant light at the end of a tunnel. Let us all, in one accord, lift high up the banner of freedom, the passion for a better Kenya flowing with justice, oneness, love, peace and abundance.

Nurture Fortitude: - Fortitude is brevity during mundane circumstances. Shepherds who leave their flock during attacks are not worth their high calling. Leaders must have a cause to live and die for. Dr Charles Blair puts it eloquently: The greatness of a man is determined by the cause he lives for and the willingness to pay the price for his achievement. Leaders are not quitters. County leaders should not be people who resign and succumb to pressure as long as they are doing the right things. Leadership is characterized by high degrees of pressure and discouragements. Leaders in our Counties must be wo/men that are willing to advance their constitutional mandate to its logical conclusion irrespective of contradictions, name-calling, being undermined and looked down upon or threats from jealous competitors.

Difficult choices must be made for the good of the county without seeking petty popularity for a second term in office. No one in recent history has depicted this sort of courage more than President Barrack Obama with his health care plan for all Americans. He knew it risked his popularity but chose to stand for what is right. General Douglas MacArthur made difficult choices at times against congressional wishes to salvage the Korean War from escalating further. Even at the county level, leadership must be development conscious and not pursue popular moves that may retard the county's general good. This calls for the spirit of fortitude.

Visionary: - Vision is the ideal situation. A leader must visualize the ideal situation in her county. She must visualize the economic position, health situation, moral values, environmental standards and educational levels that her county will realize by the end of her constitutional term in office. She may not realize all these goals. However, she will work towards this ideal scenario like climbing a high mountain. In mountaineering, there are many challenges including thick forests, ferocious beasts, low temperatures, high pressures and slippery rocks. However, with every new vantage point, there are beautiful sceneries to behold long before reaching the peak. This is vision. Enjoying the journey but keeping focus on the ideal.

Martin Luther King Jr had a dream that his four children will never be judged after their color pigmentation but the content of their character. The man died at a prime age of 38 and his vision seemed shattered. But was it? Today icons of peace like Rev Jesse Jackson enjoy the toils of King Jr and I believe President Barrack Obama epitomizes the fruition of that dream. The man died but the vision lives on. Leadership must embrace visions that long outlive its lifespan. We must see far into the future and shape the world accordingly. Leaders ought to be clear with the world they want to deliver to forthcoming generations when their eyes close down and mortal lives cease. This is called vision – the ability to see clearly into the future.

Prepare to Work: - It's Zig Ziglar who once said, 'Work is the price we pay to travel the highway of success'. Failure to plan implies planning to fail. Nothing ventured, nothing gained. Work has no substitute. Leaders must have their sleeves rolled up and get down to work. They must decide what they want to sacrifice; the price they want to pay to realize their goals. County success can never be realized by doing business as usual: politicking! County success stories will be built by those who realize that work is the foundation of all business, the parent of genius and the seed of the sower. Work has laid down the foundation of the greatest fortunes and has been the father of all empires. Leaders ought to itemize their job descriptions and a clear calendar of events closely monitored by the county residents. The leader's diary should be predetermined with a clear plan of action. No longer should we allow hap hazard leadership approaches to public assignments.

Work is not demonstrated by talking but by measurable milestones. Leadership must distinguish between activities and accomplishments; processes and results. When a horse dies in Kenya, we constitute a committee of inquiry to carry investigation on the causes of the dead horse; then consultants to look into the committees of the dead horse; then hire a new horse rider; then buy a new whip; then look for another dead horse to assist in resuscitating the dead horse; but the horse is still dead! Processes. At the meantime, the leadership term of office is gone. Hence we need clearly stipulated work schedules, indicators of achievements and monitoring of performance on a continually basis rather than waiting to evaluate at the end of the electoral term. If within a governor's term of office performance lacks, the electorate should re-call such a leader.

Persist during difficulties: - Leaders don't quit especially when everything is going wrong. Naturally people will criticize leaders almost always; whether they are right or not. As a leader, especially the county governor, one must be ready to carry on the duties of that office to its constitutional completion. This does not imply head headedness previously witnessed by some Kenyan leaders who will never resign even after gross public outcry and loss of confidence due to mischievous leadership with overwhelming evidence. Nelson Mandela's fight against apartheid for 27 years best demonstrates persistence. By handing over the Presidency mantle after only one term in office sent unequivocal message to the world on the genuineness of his struggles for his country. At the production of this publication, he remains the world's number one brand due to his persistence to the extent he laid down his own life for his country.

The Chinese bamboo tree is watered and fertilized for five years in a row without any sign of shooting until about the sixth week of the fifth year. County leaders must appreciate that there will be times and seasons that they will water and fertilize the county garden of opportunities without realizing tangible results for some taxing period. They however must persist on doing the right projects in the right way. The greatest difference between winners and losers is the ability to hold on. The real measure of faith is the ability to hang on. We must look for leaders who are resilient and emotionally stable to persist through all turmoil to deliver results for their people. Leaders who will bring together members of the county assembly from varying political persuasions and help them focus on the larger county agenda. What a shame the physical brutalities witnessed in our city hall time and again? Are these counselors leaders by any stretch of the imagination? One who cannot withstand pressure generated in round table deliberations can as well lead the people into killing en-masse and does not deserve leadership positions. Resilience and persistence must characterize our new crop of leadership.

Possess integrity: - No longer can we afford empty rhetoric. Words spoken must be bankable. As the writer has observed in one of his publications, 'The Power of The Spoken Word', words have incredible power to encourage or discourage in unbelievable manner and degree. As a country, we are used to all sorts of pronouncements prior to elections which are hardly followed for implementation. Sadly, the pronouncers have no conscious. This ought to end. Leaders must be put to spell out their intents in a solid plan of action before assuming office. Periodic reviews ought to be carried against their pledges and the recall clause must remain an open option. At the end of every term, an end term review ought to be carried out and the officers brought to account not only through the power of the ballot box but also in our courts of law if need be. Then and only then can we have men and women of integrity leading our counties which is the most critical requisite for both the county and National progress.

According to estimates published in the Financial Times on June 1, 2010, at least $854 billion has been siphoned from Africa since 1970 in capital flight. African countries surely face a crisis of leadership and governance owing to dysfunctional ethos. Loss of integrity consciousness has made leadership on this part of the world a refuge for fringe members of the elite who use abject widespread poverty as a source of lucre. Such elite leaders conspire to cannibalize the local economies and retain the perquisites of power ranging from hefty bank accounts in tax havens, private jets, weaponry, foreign property investments and the state of the art luxury cars and the like. We congratulate global leaders for confisticating and freezing Muammar Gaddafi's treasures. Certainly such massive assets belong to the Libyan people.

Why would our insurance companies hike the cover premiums for private cars to a minimum of 7.5% overnight and the NHIF wake up one morning to an unrealistic public burden? Why must one have a billion shillings to run a bank or insurance business in Kenya? There could be many reasons, some genuine and valid. However, the predominant reason, in my view, is to raise the entry barrier to new entrants and at the same time safeguard the interests of the greedy political elite who control majority shares in almost all the insurance companies and local banks by scaring off competition. I solemnly call upon the Kenyan people to critically screen the integrity of the leadership with the rise of the county system of government. We must seek to constitute level playing ground for all to encourage new business ventures that have been sidelined at the greed of monopoly by selfish leaders.

Understand peoples' plight: - Leaders must understand the issues. They must synthesize the daily agonies their constituents are going through. They must comprehend the dynamitic and complexity of the radically changing times. We need to look out for leaders who also comprehend global standards and have the capacity to lead their counties to world recognition. They must be in position to present their people's plight at any level, national or international to the extent that any audience will perceive them as understanding the issues on the ground that they presume to present. It would be disastrous, for instance, for the world to be discussing about climate change, and a leader desirous to be a county governor has no earthly idea what the animal is all about. County leaders should be in position to develop proposals that can solicit for development funding off shore for their people.

The county leaders must fully understand the Millennial Development Goals since their constituencies are a part of the global village. They need not necessarily be experts in all fields but must have a relative understanding of the current expectations of a leader in today's world. One ought to be well versed with issues affecting our planet including the effects of the arms proliferation, effects of the economies of neighboring countries, the state of the peace-less Somali, the nuclear plants debate surrounding Iran, the Middle East process, the effects of aids and grants, health plans in other parts of the world etc. A leader must see how all these parts make a whole and their direct as well as long term effects on their counties.

Protect their constituents: - Leaders must feel the emotions of the people. We are not just logical people but also emotional human beings. There will be very particular issues that are unique to a given county. However, most issues are similar in one way or another. Nonetheless, tackling the handling of small arms may need totally different approach between Turkana county and Bungoma county. The county senator must articulate this complex social dilemma that his/her constituency may face in the upper house. Leading a bloody attack like the infamous Wagalla massacre would compromise the entire bill of rights as well as the spirit of the constitution that we now have.

Efficiency is doing things right. Effectiveness is doing the right things efficiently. Our leaders should be effective. This calls for protecting the emotional part of their constituents. As such, county leaders must not just seek to do things right but also to do the right things. That is, to incorporate the subjective issues in the constituency and not just the objective ones. Leaders must empathize with the people. That is, put themselves in their shoes. This requires appreciation of multiple realities on the ground like the needs of women, youths, minorities and people living with disabilities as envisioned in our new constitution. Similarly, the un-employed, unschooled and those lost in drugs, crime and prostitution must be empathized with in view of making them self reliant individuals. Un-empathetic leaders are not worth the demanding task before them.

Role models: - Leaders should not (just) tell people what to do but lead them in what to do. The author looks forward to a time when our leadership will have strong family values as demanded in some countries. The electorate should seek to establish leaders from men and women who have high moral standing, respect the masses, detest corruption, compassionate, temperamental and peace seekers. They must lead from the front. They must learn to pass on the baton once their term of office lapses as well as prepare the next leadership for succession. We should question how wealth was acquired and not just fix people into leadership who are drug barons or have dipped their long arms illegally into public coffers. Such lifestyles though lavish contradict the very fiber of leadership.

I trust that P.L.O Lumumba together with his KACA team and the IEBC will enhance that voter bribery is a vice of the gone generation. A leader who bribes voters believes in corruption and thus fails the test of role modeling. County leadership must remain above board for true positive change to reach one and all in Kenya. A good role model is one whose words in public and his private life are inseparable. One who recognizes that people expect and respect him for being principled. Our political parties henceforth should evolve along ideological lines. At the moment they are merely vehicles to give MPs a ride to parliament and can be ditched once the mission is accomplished. This must change and shape our political parties on principle grounds.

Good communicators: - Our leadership must be able to inspire action through the power of the spoken word. The county governors and senators as well as the parliamentarians and civic leaders of necessity must be good communicators. We haven't had a problem in eloquence, Per se, but substance. We have witnessed our public rallies characterized by not very well thought out speeches especially during electoral campaigns. We have seen the majority of our contesters seeking to impress the majority unschooled populace since, as they say, politics is about numbers. We however need to grow out of this retarded notion and sojourn towards bringing life to our public debates. We need to make it compulsive for candidates seeking public offices to undergo public scrutiny through debates that are issues based.

We must congratulate our media columnists for their candid articulacy of issues affecting the populace. Our people from far and wide the country over need also to mature up and judge political characters based both on the substance of their promises, the articulacy of their action plans as well as the history of their character and development records. We cannot be good communicators unless and until we are good listeners. Leaders must intently listen to their people to really know what are the desired outputs, outcomes and impacts. After which they must articulate to the voters they are wooing on the logical steps that they will carry to bring about county development.

Connect with people: - To 'connect' means to create the time. Over the years, we have seen parliamentarians retreat to their Nairobi comfort after elections just to re-surface nearing elections. Intuitively, they must attend to their duties at the National Assembly – no argument on this matter. The extreme absentia from the constituents however by some leaders need microscopic scrutiny by the very people they claim to present. Ideally, governors, senators and parliamentarians should reside in the constituencies they present and a Nairobi home should be subordinate to the *roots* home; unless, of course, if one presents a Nairobi constituency.

If I were the President of Kenya, I would occasionally have a genuine meet-the-people tour in all counties and not only to comprehend the issues on the ground but also connect with the people. I have never known why leaders' diaries will accommodate impromptu happenings like attending deaths of prominent nationalities and cannot deliberately plan to meet the people on development agenda not tied with votes. Jacob Zuma of South Africa, for instance, has a direct line from which he receives calls from the public he serves. I salute our Prime Minister, Raila Odinga for his deliberate efforts to meet the people. I hope that our county leaders will live, work and connect with the people they earnestly seek to 'serve' during electioneering.

We are what we repeatedly do. Excellence then, is not an act, but a habit - Aristotle

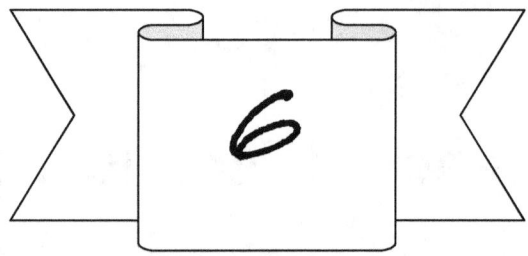

Benchmarking County Success

Harry Emerson Fosdick once said, "No horse ever gets anywhere until he is harnessed. No steam or gas ever drives anything until it is confined. No Niagara is ever turned into light and power until it is tunneled. No life ever grows great until it is focused, dedicated and disciplined." The new constitution is not an end on its own. It must be owned, nurtured and implemented for the ripe fruits it promises to be reached. Someone taught Carey Francis 2 + 2 = 4

86

before he learnt 2,465 * 6,782 = 16,717,630. We must embrace learning for us to avoid an epic march to a constitutional nirvana.

We need to benchmark from effective county governments and learn from their past mistakes and successes. To benchmark is not to copy. Benchmarking means studying the best practices and innovatively applying them in the local context. Kenya need not invent the wheel in the establishment of the devolved governance structures. From our history, centralizing governance undermines democratic governance and reduces the overall capacity of any government to cope with public demands as well as alienates the populace from their government.

The county government as advanced by the Kenyan constitution, for all practical purposes, is *federalism* as much as we don't get psyched up by this debatable terminology. In constitutional theory, no pure systems of governance exist. Federalism as well is classified as dual federalism and cooperative federalism. Dual federalism assumes a proper and distinctive relationship between the states and national government. Those who postulate it believe that the national government rule has a limited set of constitutional purposes. Each government unit – national and state – is sovereign in its own domain. This type of arrangement, usually, is rife with tension.

Cooperative federalism, on the other hand, assumes that both state (county in the Kenyan case) and nation have similar roles that intertwine and overlap. Reduced to a doctrine, it advocates joint as opposed to exclusive action, routine sharing of power and fragmentation of power, hence reducing its concentration at any of the two levels. In my considered opinion, the Kenyan system seems more inclined to cooperative federalism. Our governance structures overlap in roles and functionalities in many aspects and are interdependent. That's why the judiciary and security apparatus, by and large, are under the watch of the central government. Has this model worked elsewhere and what possible lessons are there to bench mark to enhance success?

In the summer of 2010, China became the world's second largest economy after the United States. China's rise has vital lessons that Kenya can use to benchmark at this point in time. The rise has been as a result of a combination of initiatives, but the most crucial has been a thirst for knowledge and a new willingness to engage the world on every level. During the initial rise of Chinese civilization which goes way back to 2,300 years ago, emperors built ships that were larger than anything ever constructed. The Chinese were seen in distant harbors around the world. Last year (2010), some Chinese explorers docked in Malindi to trace the relations between their mediaeval with East Africans.

But subsequent Chinese rulers decided that this exploration was too costly, and they withdrew from the world. As a result, Chinese, who had invented gun powder, had to import Europeans to show the Chinese army how to fire canons. Today, China engages the world in new ways. Most Chinese speak English to have a vantage point in reaching the global market. They rarely get involved in governance issues of the countries they are doing business with unlike the West. Here in Kenya, many people notice the Chinese presence due to their expansive infrastructural works. The story is the same in Southern Sudan, Zimbabwe and the East African Community. The tentacles of the Chinese empire stretch throughout Africa and into unlikely places like Iraq and Afghanistan building roads and health care facilities.

The People's Republic of China was founded by the Communist Party of China which is the leader of the Chinese people. The socialist system led by the working class and based on the alliance of the workers and farmers is the fundamental system of the

People's Republic of China. All the power in the country belongs to the people who exercise their power through the National People's Congress and local people's congresses at all levels. The people manage the state, economy, culture and other social affairs through a multitude of means and forms.

The fundamental task and goals of the state are to concentrate on the socialist modernization drive along the road of building socialism with Chinese characteristics; to adhere to the socialist road, persist in the reform and opening up program, improve the socialist system in all aspects, develop the market economy, expand democracy, and improve the rule of law; to be self-reliance and work hard to gradually realize the modernization of the industry, agriculture, national defense, science and technology so as to build China into a strong and democratic socialist country with a high degree of cultural development.

Although China is a one party state, its development records defies description. What has been the secret of the Chinese model? First, development is people driven. China has raised an overwhelmingly large number of prosperous middle class. Secondly technology; nowhere else do you find cutting edge technology. Thirdly, they concentrate on economic partnerships with countries around the world rather than dictating policies. Fourthly, they have sent a new signal of openness to the world by allowing all religions to operate freely. Fifthly, adequate labor force since the country still harbors great reservoirs of labor force who work for lower wages. The Chinese coastal areas however have enjoyed prosperity for some time now and are being turned into high-tech centers where workers will enjoy higher pay to focus on more complex tasks.

China reformed from the ancient dynasties, to extreme authoritarian communism rule to the current democratic space characterized by voting rights, religious freedoms and human rights which for long have been a preserve of the West like freedom of association and expression. Transportation is booming. Bullet trains are being built at record speed, and passengers' race between major cities in hours. The total length of expressway was 74,000 km (46,000 mi) at the end of 2010, second only to the United States. China has also the world's longest high-speed rail network with over 4,618 mi (7,432 km) of service routes which 601 mi (967 km) of them has been serving with train with top speed of 220 mph. Airports are being modernized at an unbelievable clip, and there are not usual waiting lines experienced elsewhere. Moreover, China is leading the world in developing nuclear energy plants using the latest technology.

From its founding in 1949 to late 1978, the People's Republic of China was a Soviet-style centrally planned economy. Private businesses and capitalism did not exist. To propel the country towards a modern, industrialized communist society, Mao Zedong instituted the Great Leap Forward. Following Mao's death and the end of the Cultural Revolution, Deng Xiaoping and the new Chinese leadership began to reform the economy and move to a market-oriented mixed economy under one-party rule. In 1978, China and Japan had normalized diplomatic relations and China had decided to borrow money from Japan in soft loans. Since 1978, Japan has been the main foreign donor for China. China's economy is mainly characterized as a market economy based on private property ownership. Collectivization of the agriculture was dismantled and farmlands were privatized to increase productivity.

A wide variety of small-scale enterprises were encouraged while the government relaxed price controls and promoted foreign investment. Foreign trade was focused upon as a major vehicle of growth, which led to the creation of Special Economic Zones (SEZs) first in Shenzhen (near Hong Kong) and then in other Chinese cities. Inefficient state-owned enterprises (SOEs) were restructured by introducing western-style management system and the unprofitable ones were closed, resulting in massive job losses. Since economic liberalization began in 1978, the PRC's investment- and export-led economy has grown 90 times bigger and is the fastest growing major economy in the world. According to IMF that PRC's annual average GDP growth for the period of 2001-2010 was 10.5 percent and predicted to grow with 9.5 percent for the period of 2011-2015. As Global Growth Generators countries announced by Citigroup at February 2011, China had high 3G Index. It now has the world's second largest nominal GDP at 39.8 trillion yuan (US$6.05 trillion).

The clear lessons that county governments can learn from the Chinese model are: to seek for economic partnerships locally and off shore, accommodate divergent views from constituents, incorporate innovation in problem solving, be determined to be the best in class in all fields of endeavor, adopt technology in management and enhance infrastructural growth to speed up development. County leaders must be willing to travel to model economies and seek to learn lessons that rejuvenated the Chinese productivity. Two lessons from the Chinese model must be retaliated. First, they reformed their economic management system and modeled from the West modern practices. Secondly, development was not taken to the people but rather, the people were the drivers of the economy. The years there was too much government in private lives the Chinese economy was either on plateau or sank into doldrums. When the government liberalized the economy and empowered the people, development sprung forth like a never failing spring.

In the U.S., a county is a local level of government below the state or federal territory. Counties are in 48 of the 50 states; Louisiana is divided into parishes and Alaska into boroughs. Currently, there are 3,143 counties and county-equivalents. Independent cities, which are not part of the county, are different from consolidated city-counties, where a city and county are merged into one unified jurisdiction and is simultaneously a city and a county, having powers and responsibilities of both types of entities.

Similarly in the Kenyan case, the county governments can create lower governance units. This is where the current town and municipal councils can have a legally safe haven as sub units answerable to the county government as provided for in article 176 (2) and schedule 6 section 18. Article 176 (2) provides: "Every county government shall decentralize its functions and the provision of its services to the extent that is efficient and practicable to do so." Article 18 of our constitution directs parliament to pass legislation to provide for the governance of urban areas and cities since they are run differently from rural counties. This legislation will shed the light on how governance of cities and major towns will be done. However, on a comparative analysis, the different usage of the terminology *county* aside, the counties in the Kenyan case compare with the federal states in the U.S. functionally.

There is much we can benchmark from the United States constitution that Thomas Jefferson authored in 1776. When President John F. Kennedy honored 49 Nobel laureates in the early 1960s, he said the gathering was the greatest collection of genius ever at the white house – except for one occasion. And that, said Kennedy, was when Thomas Jefferson dined alone. J.F.K. must have referred to the writing of the Declaration of Independence by Jefferson which was signed in Philadelphia.

Here was a leader who went the extra mile for his people. Indeed when Jefferson wrote the words for his own gravestone, he left the fact that he was a two-term president of the United States. He died on July 4, 1826 but his legacy lives on. This is the man who declared sternly on U.S. soil that all men are created equal and have some inalienable rights among these are liberty, freedom and the pursuit of happiness. This has since become the cornerstone of the U.S. fraternity upon which civil rights movements rode upon.

Although Kenya has moved away from a unitary system, its constitutional architects' stress that it remains unitary which by another name is cooperative federalism in constitutional theory. Rather than construct a federal system, Otiende Amollo of the Committee of Experts said that they wanted to deconstruct a unitary system. The devolved system thus has fundamental differences from the U.S system with the Kenyan counties weaker than the U.S. States. However, the national and legislative branch resembles the U.S. system. Each of the 50 U.S. States is represented by two senators in the upper house (Senate) while the number of representatives elected from each State to the House of Representatives is determined by the population. Our counties however cannot maintain separate police forces and they lack provision for local judiciary. The practicability of devolving such institutions at the county level should be food for thought for posterity planning.

Isn't Kenya blessed? Kenya is sub-Saharan Africa's second biggest economy, behind only South Africa despite the fact that we are not very endowed with natural resources save the grit and ingenuity of our people. We are also the seventh population wise lagging behind Nigeria, Ethiopia, Democratic Republic of Congo, South Africa, Sudan and Tanzania. From World Bank's figures of 2009, our overall GDP is nearly double that of Uganda, Six times that of Rwanda and twenty one times that of Burundi. These successes have been achieved in the absence of a devolved structure of government. This is simply because it is people who produce results and not systems. Thus the goodwill of the Kenyan people and the leadership thereof holds the secret of our country's better and more hopeful future rather than governance structures.

Good as it sounds on face value; the federal government has never been the end key to success anywhere. Much less in Nigeria whose federal legislature is the bicameral assembly comprising the Senate and the House of representatives. The Senate is made up of three senators each from the 36 states and one from the federal capital territory of Abuja bringing the total to 109. On the other hand is the House of Representatives consisting of 360 members elected from single member constituencies. The Nigerian federal structure of governance borrows heavily from the U.S. model with three tiers: federal, state and local with the executive power vested in the President who appoints ministers with the senate's approval.

Each of the states in Nigeria has a unicameral legislature, the House of Assembly, responsible for making state laws which must be consistent with federal laws. The executive power in each state is vested in the state governor and runs a state civil service. Each state enacts laws to set up local councils and provides for their structure, composition, finances and functions necessary to meet both economic and social progress of the state. But despite such a devolved structure of government, the Nigerian system has left 70% of its 150 million population below the poverty line according to World's Fact Book, 2010.

Although military rule that has dominated at least 30 years of independent Nigeria and overdependence on oil exports may explain the economic situation; by and large, the progress of Nigeria has been deterred by lack of intergovernmental consultation and coordination, the overlapping of duties and the weak resources of local governments. For instance, in the maintenance of law and order, state governors have complained that the state commissioners of police ignore them and take orders from the Federal Inspector General, even though the governor of the state is the chief law officer. Similarly, the local government officials have been patronized by state officers especially where local government chairmen come from different parties with the state governors.

Lack of official consultations has been wanting in the current grand coalition government. The stalemate in the appointment of Justice Alnashir to be the Chief Justice, Prof Githu Muigai to be the Attorney General, Kioko Kilukumi to be the Director of Public Prosecutions and William Kirwa to the post of Controller of Budget explain the grave crisis in our public consultations in high offices. If consultations within a central government can get so politicized, one can be forgiven for being overly concerned with how development efforts will get concerted between the central and county governments in the light of multi-party composition of public servants. The way out is to confront this obvious challenge upfront and long before it knocks in the corridors of power at both levels of government.

Pros and cons of federal governance – the Indian case
India is currently a Federal Republic. The Indian Constitution is the supreme law and any rule which violates fundamental rights is unconstitutional and hence void. The Government of India, officially known as the Union Government and also known as the Central Government is the governing authority of a union of 28 states and seven union territories, collectively called the Republic of India and is seated in India's capital, New Delhi.

95

The government comprises three branches: the executive, the legislative and the judiciary. The government of India is elected democratically. Eligible voters may vote at the polling station in his/her constituency at which he /she is registered on presentation of the voter's identity card or other suitable identification. Use of electronic voting machines has simplified the process of voting and counting. 84 out of 543 seats in parliament are reserved to various social groups and tribes, while the large majorities are open and unrestricted. In local elections, 33% of the seats are reserved for women. The Election Commission of India is responsible for ensuring free and fair elections.

The executive branch is headed by the President, who is the Head of State and republic and is elected by an electoral college indirectly for a term of five years. The executive power is vested mainly on the President of India (Article 53(1)) who acts in consultation with the head of government, the Prime Minister of India and his or her Council of Ministers - the cabinet (Article 74). All the members of the Council of Ministers as well as the Prime Minister are members of Parliament. If they are not, they must be elected within a period of six months from the time they assume their respective office. The Prime Minister and the Council of Ministers are accountable to the Lok Sabha (lower house of parliament), individually as well as collectively. If there is a policy failure or lapse on the part of the government, all the members of the council are jointly responsible. If a vote of no confidence is passed against the government, then all the ministers headed by the Prime Minister have to resign.

Every individual minister is in charge of a specific ministry or ministries (or specific other portfolio). He is responsible for any act of failure in all the policies relating to his department. In case of any lapse, he himself is individually responsible to the Parliament. If a vote of no confidence is passed against the individual minister, he has to resign. Individual responsibility can amount to collective responsibility. Therefore, the Prime Minister, in order to save his government, can ask for the resignation of such a minister like the way Shashi tharoor was forced to resign by Prime Minister Dr. Manmohan singh.

India has a parliamentary system of government largely resembling that of the United Kingdom (Westminster system). The legislature is the Parliament which is bicameral in nature, consisting of two houses: the directly-elected 545-member Lok Sabha - House of the People- the lower house and the 250-member indirectly-elected and appointed Rajya Sabha - Council of States - the upper house. Lok Sabha could be compared with our national assembly while Rajya is comparable to our senate except that in the Kenyan case the senators are directly elected by the people.

The judiciary consists of the Supreme Court of India and 21 High Courts at the state level, and District and Session Courts at the district level. Unlike its US counterpart, the Indian justice system consists of a unitary system at both state and federal level. The Supreme Court of India has original, appellate and advisory jurisdiction and consists of a Chief Justice and 30 associate justices, all appointed by the President on the advice of the Chief Justice of India. Just like the Kenyan case, the supreme court's exclusive original jurisdiction extends to any dispute between the Government of India and one or more states, or between the Government of India and any state or states on one side and one or more states on the other, or between two or more states, if and insofar as the dispute involves any question (whether of law or of fact) on which the existence or extent of a legal right depends.

The combination of corruption and politics plays a key role in governance. In 2009, nearly a quarter of the 543 elected members of parliament had been charged with crimes, including rape or murder. There are many institutional efforts such as the Right to Information Act, computerization/e-Governance, the establishment of Lokayukta to check corruption. This has however not yielded much of the required results because the Indian government is among the most bureaucratic in the world. The current government has concluded that most spending fails to reach its intended recipients. Lant Pritchett calls India's public sector "one of the world's top ten biggest problems - of the order of AIDS and climate change".

The Economist article about Indian civil service (2008) said that Indian central government employs around 3 million people and states another 7 million, including "vast armies of paper-shuffling peons". The Economist states that "India has some of the hardest-working bureaucrats in the world, but its administration has an abysmal record of serving the public". Unannounced visits by government inspectors showed that 25% of public sector teachers and 40% of public sector medical workers could not be found at the workplace. Teacher absence rates ranged from 15% in Maharashtra to 71% in Bihar. Despite worse absence rates, public sector teachers enjoy salaries at least five times higher than private sector teachers. India's absence rates are among the worst in the world.

Many experiments with computerization have failed due to corruption and other factors. In 2008, Tanmoy Chakrabarty noted that "There are vested interests everywhere; politicians fear that they will lose control with e-government, and this is coming in the way of successful implementation of e-government projects in India. Out of the 27 projects under the NEGP, only one (the MCA21 program) has been completed. There is tremendous gap between conceptualization and implementation".

98

Although the government subsidizes everything from gasoline to food, much of the effort is lost through corrupt systems. Loss-making state-owned enterprises are supported by the government. Farmers are given electricity for free. Overall, a 2005 article by International Herald Tribune stated that subsidies amounted to 14% of GDP. As much as 39 percent of subsidized kerosene is stolen. Moreover, these subsidies cause economic distortions. On the other hand, India spends relatively little on education, health, or infrastructure. Urgently needed infrastructure investment has been much lower than in China. According to the UNESCO, India has the lowest public expenditure on higher education per student in the world. As per the CIA World Factbook, India ranks 23rd in the world with respect to the Public Debt with a total of 61.30% of GDP just before United states which ranks 24th (2008 estimated).

As much as India has a devolved system of governance, corruption has eaten into all levels of government undermining the country's potential. Lack of accountability characterizes public service where government workers pretend to work. Worse still are government subsidies that kill intuition and individual industry. Many Indians as a result are over reliant on the government. People must always learn that there is no short cut to hard work. How tragic that some leaders incited Kibera residents not to pay rent during the 2007/2008 mayhem. No government schemes and determination will substitute individuals' hard work. county leaders must instill the culture of hard work amongst their constituents. This chiefly has been the secret of China and Japan's economic progress. Hard work, integrity, consistency and a determination to succeed and not devolved structures pays off.

In Kenya, the greed of monopoly has always attempted to corrupt government structures in favor of the favorite few at the expense of the majority. For instance, the Ministry of Roads demands one to have constructed several roads and bought heavy equipment and machinery prior to being registered as a construction company with the Ministry. Besides, one is required to produce audited accounts for the last three years and to have recruited engineers to serve in his company that is yet to start. How would an interested small scale investor venture into the construction industry? How would one even purchase such expensive machinery and hire expensive workforce before he is even registered by the Ministry in the first place? Their counterpart, the Ministry of Public Works makes similar demands before registering a company to be allowed to engage in construction of buildings and public works. The story is the same at the Ministry of Water and Irrigation for a company to be registered to dig dams and boreholes.

All this is done to block new entrants into the industry which by any other name is institutionalized corruption. Legislations that favor monopoly and destroy the opportunities for small scale ventures perhaps explain the widening gap between the haves and have-nots in Kenya more than any other factor. The Directorate of Industrial Training (DIT) under the Ministry of labor will not register an individual unless s/he has an acceptable office – the definition of acceptable remains their prerogative which also includes acceptable office locality. I have often wondered why a qualified university professor needs an extra private office to be registered to train in this country when their counterparts in Japan operate from their houses. DIT officers argue that they defend their clients from unscrupulous traders – companies soliciting for training – quite interesting! Their vetting criteria defies reason and demonstrates the corrupt legislations that hinder new comers into business while jealously guarding the large corporate players to dominate over the majority small scale ventures. Nothing perpetuates poverty any more.

The requirements for starting a training institution or a school under the Ministry of Education as well as higher education are prohibitive against beginners. The banking, insurance, the microfinance sectors and all financial institutions have demands that small business owners can at most just dream about. I find no difference between official graft as we know it in Kenya with legislations that protect a small class of elites enjoying deliberate government monopoly structures at the expense of the majority. Today, you cannot do any business with the government before you show case where you have done projects of similar magnitudes in the past. This is in line with PPOA act, regulations and procedures. One cannot but wonder how a new entrant will do the first project no matter how qualified a beginner might be.

A visiting coffee dealer was shocked to see coffee growers unable to meet their basic needs like quality health care and education for their children. He couldn't fathom the poverty surrounding the small scale growers of coffee bearing in mind that in his country, the United States, they use 1% of the Kenyan coffee to blend the Robusta they import from Latin America. That's how dear our coffee is over yonder. So is our tea and horticulture among many other products. Basic registration to be a coffee dealer in Kenya costs USD 1,000. To register a Trust, NGO, Society or a club is a nightmare in Kenya. Registrations surrounding oil importation and dealership are no reach for the commoner. We ought to challenge the economic structures that discourage new ventures and safeguard cartels. By making the business environment investor friendly and fair ground for all, we will witness the populace driving the economy robustly.

These are structures that our county governments must confront from the very onset to take development to the people; else, we will just devolve corruption. Whoever will have the privilege of sitting in our county assemblies need to stand out to counted to safeguard the interests of the small scale farmer and business owner against policies and local legislations that will favor the minority few at the expense of the majority. We ought to learn these lessons from the Indian case and avoid the same pitfalls that propagate misery among our people. County leadership must advocate for policies that will give fair and equal opportunities to all county members especially to the small scale business owners since the big corporate players will continue to do business with the central government. Indeed, county legislations should be drafted in such a manner that they give leverage to the genuine locals in all public procurements.

The Indian case has some positive aspects to learn from. If a cabinet minister acts in contravention to the law, s/he can resign on her/his own volition. Should s/he not, the head of the government, the Prime Minister can prevail upon such an individual to resign from office. Should the Prime Minister and the Cabinet Council attempt to protect such an individual; then they will all hold collective responsibility and the entire cabinet is compelled to resign by the lower house, Lok Sabha which is directly elected by the people. This is very positive against impunity in the high offices. We could borrow a leaf and suggest that members of our County Assemblies should hold both individual and collective responsibility in service delivery to the people. Indeed, parliament should enact legislations that outline procedures of collective responsibilities that will hold county governments accountable to the electorate.

Since the new constitution is largely a blue print to guide our governance, we need to restructure our public systems to enhance equal opportunities for all citizens regardless of creed, tribe, religion, age, gender and other social affiliations. We need to deliberately protect the small scale farmer who has been the back bone of our economy against exploitation by wolfish unscrupulous middle men. At the local level, legislations should allow all sorts of legal businesses to boom including the banking, education, health, tourism and production of various industrial products and cottage industries. There is no single reason why production of yoghurt, soaps, honey, creams, juices, flours and countless other products, should be a preserve of major industrial plants due to our prohibitive legislations.

Whereas we shouldn't kill our major industries and imports, we should not at the same time lock out the small business owners from penetrating various industries because of selected prohibitive legislations. Our legislations should encourage small scale farmers from Mwea to pack rice; those from Kitale to pack maize flour; Narok to pack wheat flour; Kericho to pack tea; Mumias to pack sugar; and so on and so forth. The idea behind capitalism is to keep the country free and for individuals to be competitive with minimal government. Prices should be dictated by the natural laws of supply and demand in a free market. If a small holder grower is able to package his milk, he should be given the platform to compete with NewKCC, Tunzo, Delamere and Brookside with no undue government restrictions.

More business is lost every year through neglect than through any other cause   - Jim Cathcart

Prioritizing County Issues

Ms Dabey Maow, 36, returned home on Sunday the 10th October 2010 after 18 hours in search of a basic human need, water, as reported by Daily Nation reporters. The mother of six left home on Saturday at noon to search for water, 20 Kms away. Ms Maow, a resident of Malah Libah, 50 kilometers from Habaswein, the biggest trading center in Wajir south constituency, said she spent much of the time digging the river bed with her bare hands as she struggled to fill her jerricans being extremely watchful not to be bitten by snakes. The water can only last her a day and a half before another 20 – kilometer trek in search of water again.

Her story is replicated in many households across the expansive constituency, one of the largest in the country. Water is perhaps the major issue in this constituency followed by poverty, insecurity, illiteracy, poor infrastructures, lack of health facilities and immense food shortages. Electricity is only found at Habaswein and not a single kilometer of the road network is tarmacked. Literally, the residents say they are heading for Kenya whenever they have that rare chance to travel to Nairobi. But elections in this constituency are never issue based but clan based.

South Wajir constituents are members of the Ogaden clan with four sub clans: Bagheri, Geri, Mohamed Zuber and Makabul. Interestingly, elections of candidates into public office in this part of the world are determined by the sub clan from which one originates. This story is not unique but experienced across the country. Real issues are put on the periphery as clan and cash matters take precedence. It is Aristotle who observed: "We are what we repeatedly do. Excellence then, is not an act, but a habit". This has been Kenya since gods kept the records. But is this the Kenya of the future? Shall we ever be issue based?

Thirty years ago, then Turkana central MP Peter Ejore vigorously denied in parliament that there was famine in his home district, despite the fact that tens of thousands of his constituents were already in famine camps. In the Moi and Kenyatta era, it was almost treasonable to claim that people had died of hunger. Since, times have changed and politicians gladly highlight the sufferings of their people. Today food is politics and politics is food in Turkana. The district's three legislator's are all former employees of Oxfam and many other politicians have proven track records in emergency work as observed by writer Gabriel Dolan.

Efforts by World Food Program (WFP) to distribute food in Turkana Central have been frustrated by current local MP who insists that the Kenya Red Cross (KRC) is the leading agency in the distribution. Why wouldn't WFP and KRC compliment each other's efforts to salvage the situation? What is the area MP's interest with KRC? Are these two organizations equally sincere at their efforts? I wonder what the Turkana county will prioritize and likewise what the national government will prioritize on behalf of the Turkana people. I want to imagine that the Kitale – Lokichogio road linking the district with Southern Sudan will be prioritized to open up the area agriculturally and other business avenues. I also hope other dams like the Gibe III dam constructed on the River Omo will be done in a sustainable manner to increase livelihood.

Similarly, for Homa Bay county to reverberate economically, leadership must rise above petty partisan local politics. The six constituencies in this county: Gwassi, Mbita, Karachuonyo, Ndhiwa, Kasipul Kabondo and Rangwe span the potential of vast pineapple farms, potato farming, fisheries and the tourism potential of the Lake Victoria and the Ruma National Park. But despite all these resources in Homa Bay, the majority of the residents live in abject poverty and are subjects of severe HIV/AIDS scourge. At the meantime, their leaders are enjoying the latest whisky in a Nairobi joint; and for those who were *lucky* to have ministerial appointments, they are cutting cool deals. The next time the county issues will be articulated will be about six months to the 2012 elections.

Success is never accidental. It is planned. We have often heard that if we fail to plan, we plan to fail. What is true of an individual is true for an organization, a county and a country. As a country, we surely have brilliant blue prints like the Vision 2030, various government strategies for different ministries and progress audits.

We regularly conform to rapid based management styles by conducting regular organizational surveys like employee tracking survey, customer satisfaction surveys, work environment surveys, training needs assessment, integrity perception surveys and skills gap analysis. We also have outstanding policies like HIV/AIDS policies, people living with disabilities policies, IT policies, Communications Policies, Monitoring and Evaluation policies, HR policies and many more.

We must commend the country's leadership for such astute leadership initiatives. Some of the issues raised by these documents lag in their implementation scheduling but most of them have been implemented with high degrees of success. Unfortunately however is that many Kenyans do not appreciate sacrificial efforts that have taken place especially in the last eight years. This chapter seeks to encourage the county governments to develop right from onset clear development plans that clearly prioritize issues at the county level. This is called goal setting. It must be reiterated that the implementation of these county goals must be in line with national goals. Otherwise, conflict between the two levels of government will slow the course of reforms and progress at both levels.

In 1950, a war torn devastated Japan, a country that had lost a higher percentage of its young men to war than any other nation in the last 100 years, resolved to focus ahead. Despite the fact that they have no oil, iron, core, steel or any real natural resources; they chose not to blame game each other. Government agents, entrepreneurs and all important stake holders convened to set national goals. Every decade since the 50s, the Japanese had clear and concrete written down goals. Among the major national goals for four consecutive decades were:

- In the 1950 decade, they set to be the leading nation in the world in the production of textiles. They achieved it although they do not have Textile fibers of any kind like Wool, Cotton, Polyester, Acrylic and Nylon. They imported all the raw materials but remained focused on this priority.
- In the 1960 decade, they resolved to be the number one country in the world in the production of steel. In order to do this, they had to import core and iron thousands of miles away, put up steel mills and re-export the finished products several thousand miles away in an already highly competitive market. The Japanese did not look at what they did not have; they looked at what they did have: willingness to work, positive mental work attitude, team work and positive talk. Hard they worked and achieved this ambitious goal.

- In the 1970 decade, they decided to be the leading nation in the world in the production of automobiles. Since that declaration, the Japanese motor vehicle plants are the largest in the world and they are leading in the production of automobiles to this very day. Evident in the Toyotas, Mitsubishis and Sunnis that have saturated our country.

- Their 1980 decade goal was to be the number one country in the world in the production of electronics and computers. All you need to do is to visit the video land and the computer world today and agree that they achieved that goal.

The Japanese chose to set goals. They believed in themselves and in their leaders. The greatest challenge in our country of Kenya today is not lack of natural resources but weak faith in our

109

national visions and in the leadership. Many Kenyans neither trust their religious, administrative nor the political leaders. There is no single reason why Japan, South Korea, Singapore, Taiwan, U.A.E and Malaysia should be performing better than Kenya today if natural resources were to go by. We must learn how to set workable goals and believe in the leadership implementing our county goals.

In a separate title, `The Power of the Spoken Word', the author takes great page to discuss on the topic of patriotism in respect to the language of a patriot. In that book, the author evaluates the effect of words that we use on a day to day basis in relation to national success or failure. Towards the cause of success, the author observes that citizens must have a patriotic mindset best reflected in the positivism or negativism in the use of their day to day language. Thus, no matter how inspiring goals can be, faith must be added as a vital ingredient to a county's success.

Goal setting is a hard art. It requires courage to make a decision between all good options. Yet, this MUST be done. One of the boldest goal setter in our time is U.S president Barrack Obama. In one of the presidential debates between candidates Barrack Obama and John McCain during the U.S 2008 elections, the hopefuls were asked to prioritize between security, health and economy. John McCain gave the wisest answer of all times. Impossible to prioritize all important issues. Isn't it? One can't tell citizens to wait for security issues to be sorted out since a health care is being worked on. A September 11 might recur. Right? You can't keep the economy on hold to work out health and security issues since their success depends solely on a working economy. Correct? Sounds intellectually logical.

But I am sorry, John McCain was dead wrong! The question was: Prioritize? The interviewer knew very well that all the issues at hand were extremely important. But issues must be prioritized and leadership can't wallow in dilemma. Leaders must be decisive. Barrack Obama prioritized without blinking in his mind: Number one, health. Why? You can't offer security to a dying people due to failing health much less can you insinuate you are revitalizing the economy for a population that won't be there in the first place. Number two, security. One won't even invest when their lives and investments are in danger. Security must precede investments. Obviously the third item on the list was economy. This is leadership. President Obama took a serious risk by prioritizing all important national issues. He argued that a country, just like a family, must prioritize issues because budgets can only accommodate so much.

Hard as this may sound, a leader must prioritize issues since resources may not always allow for all items to be sorted out simultaneously. In making such decisions, a leader cannot sit on the fence. Indecisiveness at the highest office may as well explain the escalating violence that we witnessed in the 2007/8 PEV. Interestingly enough, people will follow a leader even with a few mistakes here and there based on simple understanding that leaders are humans too. Howbeit no one will follow an indecisive leader who lacks clarity of vision, purpose and direction. County leadership must be decisive in making tough developmental priorities.

Unfortunately it will go into the annals of history that the Kenyan Vice President, H.E. Hon Kalonzo Musyoka, was indecisive or perceived so by the public during the 2010 Constitution referendum. He was thus labeled a water melon which is inside 'red' and outside 'green' in accordance to the symbolic colors presenting the 'No' and the 'Yes' sides of the Constitutional debate. He wanted to appease both the naysayers and the yes-sayers concurrently. Consequence? Miserable failure in his future

111

leadership prospects and fortunes. Let's not fool ourselves; whereas Constitutional debate was a far reaching national plan; it has sure consequences for political aspirants. In life, people hate indecision. Masses will always follow leaders who fall, dust off and rise up from the ashes of defeat but they never follow indecisive leaders.

True for national leadership, true for county leadership. The nub of the matter is that County Assemblies and Executive Committees must take bold steps of setting County goals. This must be a priority in the county's strategic plan. Counties could benchmark from each other or from the international front. However, they should avoid a copy and paste pattern since it leads to generalizations. For instance, whereas security is a key ingredient to economic growth, its priority in Kiambu and Mumias counties are fundamentally different. Thus, county leadership ought to develop area-specific priorities to fit the local situation. The Dubai government announced in 2008 that fighting corruption was the major priority and true to its commitment, a number of public servants not only lost their jobs but were prosecuted on graft grounds. This was not necessarily the priority in the other Emirates in the U.A.E.

President Jacob Zuma of South Africa not long ago resolutely sacked a whooping seven members of his cabinet who were found wanting in competence and accountability issues. On the contrary in Kenya, whenever the sacred cows are implicated wanting in accountability, issues are politicized and our straightforward law made muddy by subjecting judicial functions to the whims and caprices of a quintessentially self seeking parliamentarians. *Smaller* fish are cherry picked as symbolic acolytes to die for the sins of their untouchable god fathers as was witnessed in the city council cemetery land saga. No matter how determined PLO Lumumba or any other anti-graft chief after him will be to fight corruption in the high places; without support directly from the state house echelons, this monster that has crippled our economy will but mutate to new and more trickery forms.

Case Study One: Government priorities in New South Wales in 2008
The New South Wales government had five priority areas viz:

(i) Sustainable growth in the right locations

- The right balance between jobs and the environment through comprehensive assessment of major economic developments and infrastructure projects
- Adequate land reserved and available for industry, commerce and services
- Renewal and revitalization in strategic locations like the Greater Homebush precinct, South Sydney and the Newcastle waterfront

(ii) Improved investor and community confidence

- Reforms that ensure the planning system stays responsive and relevant. The plans of the future will be more comprehensive and fewer in number
- Effective and credible development assessment process
- More community involvement in the way that plans are developed, implemented and reviewed. Local communities will be able to determine their own futures within regional plans which set out broad principles
- Better public access to information about planning. Our web site will play an important role in this

(iii) Effective management of natural, environmental and cultural resources and values

113

- Protection for the New South Wales coastline from inappropriate development through the NSW Government's Coastal Policy, State Environmental Planning Policy No. 71 - Coastal Protection, the Comprehensive Coastal Assessment and the Coastal Lands Protection Scheme. Coastal wetlands, littoral rainforests and areas with acid-sulfate soils also need special attention if development is being considered.
- Protection for other areas of high environmental value. For example, our drinking water catchment plan will protect the drinking water for Sydney and nearby regional canters

(iv) Diverse, equitable and pleasant neighborhoods which reflect community needs and aspirations

- An adequate supply of housing - in areas where people want to live and with good access to services
- Choice in housing - we plan for the needs of our changing population. Households are getting smaller, people live longer
- Affordable housing - through protection of existing low-cost rental housing, demonstration projects and inclusion of affordable housing in major renewal developments
- Good quality urban design - design quality for residential flat buildings is a specific priority. As well we provide guidelines which help councils and developers achieve well-designed neighborhoods and attractive, usable public spaces
- Livable neighborhoods - our area improvement programs revitalize town centers' and transport interchanges, fund improvements to parks and public open space, regenerate bushland, and green the urban environment

(v) Integrated delivery of regional infrastructure and government activities

- Comprehensive regional planning strategies driven by active partnerships between state and local government, communities and business
- Plans for renewal areas and new-release areas that ensure integrated delivery of infrastructure and public services such as roads, schools, water and sewerage systems, power and gas, hospitals, police and other government activities
- Coordination between transport improvements and new development. Accessible public transport will feature strongly in the communities of the future. We aim for the right businesses and services in the right locations

Case Study Two: Government priorities in the State of Indiana in 2010

Indiana General Assembly opened its 2010 session with virtually no money to spend and little time to act before lawmakers stopped working in March. Yet, even while operating under such restrictions, legislators have an opportunity to adopt several important proposals, including ethics reform. Here is The Star Editorial Board's legislative agenda for they had for 2010:

(i) More ethical government:

Even House Speaker Pat Bauer, a longtime opponent of restrictions on lobbyists' influence over legislators, now acknowledges that the Statehouse has been compromised. "It was apparent the level of pressure exerted by special interests put a cloud over the legislature's ability to respond to the concerns of Hoosiers," Bauer wrote concerning last year's session in an op-ed

115

published in The Star in November. The General Assembly should adopt five common-sense reforms to reduce the level of influence that special interests hold over lawmakers:

- Legislators may not accept any gift worth more than $50 in value from registered lobbyists.
- Lobbyists must disclose the value of goods and services offered to individual legislators or groups of lawmakers, including meals, tickets to sporting and entertainment events, or other gifts.
- Legislators may not accept gifts, including payment of travel-related expenses, from businesses, organizations or individuals that do business with the state.
- Legislators may not accept meals, tickets to athletic games or other events, or any other gift valued at more than $50 from state universities or colleges.
- Former legislators may not work as registered lobbyists until one year after they leave office.

(ii) Better representation for voters:

Lawmakers have a prime opportunity to end the discredited practice of gerrymandering ahead of redistricting in 2011. The best means to ensure fairness and impartiality in drawing district maps is to assign the job to an independent commission. It may be possible, according to research by the Brennan Center for Justice, to create such a commission without having to pursue a constitutional amendment. Legislators should create a system for drawing district maps that fosters competitive elections, encourages qualified candidates to seek elected office and protects voters' ability to make a difference on Election Day (iii)More efficient local government:

Indiana taxpayers continue to pay for far more government than they need. In a year when state and local budgets are squeezed tight, townships are still sitting on more than $200 million in reserves. If they were ready to put the public's best interests ahead of their political allies' concerns, lawmakers would finally eliminate township government this year. That's not likely to happen, however. Instead, legislators at least need to trim around the edges by adopting three modest reforms:

- Township advisory boards should be abolished. It's a step that would save taxpayers money without sacrificing oversight or transparency.
- Poor relief, now dispensed inefficiently and unevenly by 1,008 township trustees, should be consolidated on the county level, a move that likely would improve service and reduce costs.
- School board elections should be shifted from the May primary to the general election in November to assure better voter turnout and raise the profile of these important races.

(iv)A cleaner environment:

In a state where air and water quality rank among the worst in the nation, environmental initiatives deserve far more attention than they have received from the General Assembly and the governor. One measure that could help promote use of wind and solar power involves so-called net metering, which allows consumers to send excess power that they generate back onto the electrical grid.

117

Legislators should increase the current 10-kilowatt cap on net metering to 1,000 kilowatts.

(v) Better schools:

Modest steps are again the most likely avenues for progress, in this instance because of a lack of money. One proposal that deserves strong bipartisan support centers on closing loopholes that allow abusive teachers to escape accountability. Lawmakers should ensure that school districts have access to all the information they need about a prospective employee's background before they make a hire. The legislature also should eliminate off-the-record agreements that allow districts to remove substantiated reports of misconduct from employees' files without conducting a formal hearing.

Safer children: The General Assembly achieved a welcome advancement last year when it set up an office of ombudsman to make the Department of Child Services more accountable to the public. Now, legislators should give the ombudsman the necessary resources, including sufficient legal authority, to make a real difference

How to set county Priorities

Priorities should chiefly be based on Value, Cost, and Risk. On a small project, the stakeholders can probably agree on requirement priorities informally. Larger or more contentious projects need a more structured approach, which removes some of the emotion, politics, and guesswork from prioritization. Industry analysts have proposed several techniques that involve estimating the relative value and relative cost of each requirement, such that the highest priority requirements provide the largest fraction of the total product/service value at the smallest fraction of the total cost. In essence, you're trying to identify those requirements that will maximize the product/service value within the existing cost constraints. Subjectively estimating the cost and value by pair-wise comparisons of all the requirements is impractical for anything more than a couple dozen projects.

The county executive can make use of various project management tools to help setting priorities right for more complex projects. Some of which include the PERT (Project Evaluation Review Technique) method, critical path analysis, work scheduling, Gantt charts, various numeric methods in determining the worth of a project like Net Present Value, payback period, discounted payback and Average Rate of Returns. There are also several non-numeric methods that can be explored like cost benefit analysis, comparative advantage, competitive necessity, operating necessity and product line extension. Softwares now exist to help make such work easier to execute. Professionals in IT and Project Management should be hired to help in assisting the county leadership in setting priorities right, implementing as well monitoring and evaluating project progress and overall county mission.

It is not in the author's interest to get technical in this subject but to emphasize the vitality of county governments setting priorities due to the complexity of their customers. One simple method that leadership in the County Assemblies can employ in setting priorities is categorizing projects as high, medium and low. The high ones are a mission critical; the medium ones are necessary but could wait; while the low ones are quality enhancers and can be carried out if resources would permit. Still the leadership can classify priorities into three major categories: essential, conditional and optional. Essential implies that the project must be done and performance will be unacceptable without its completion; conditional would enhance the county's mission while optional may or may not be worthwhile.

All these priorities must be in line with the county's strategic plan. Failure to plan ahead will imply adhoc approach to projects. Moreover, future county leaders will thrash ongoing projects to frustrate the works of their predecessors as has been the case in Kenya for political gain. But when the plans are laid down, leadership's role is to implement the county mission without diversionary political tactics. In my view, development, by and large, should be left for the County Executive with minimal supervision from the County Assembly. The more the political class interferes with the technical team, the less the county achieves her goals. The county goals must likewise conform to the national goals and not conflict. The national and county governments should compliment and not conflict. Thus, while setting out local goals, the county leadership must be guided by national interests.

I
t is amazing what you can accomplish if you do not care who gets the credit – Harry Truman

Succession Leadership

President Harry S Truman once said, "It is amazing what you can accomplish if you do not care who gets the credit". I wonder how many leaders would make financial contributions in a *harambee* where they won't get recognized. If one is philanthropic enough to pay fees for a needy child, why must he shout at house tops? It is this idea of seeking praise and fame that makes our leadership destroy the platform for incoming leaders. Similarly, the incoming leaders destroy the already laid down foundations by their predecessors just to deny them the glory they deserve as the project initiators. Consequently, we have a severe weakness in grooming leadership; an attitude that leads to growth retardation.

As a continent, we have lessons we can draw from former Ghanaian President, John Kufuor on planning for succession leadership. He sees leadership in Africa as having evolved linearly from the freedom fighter leadership that took over the reins of power from the departing colonialists, to the current leadership that he defines as transformational in his reading of African leadership. The freedom fighter leadership was characterized by individuals who made gallant sacrifices and took personal risks to win freedom for their people.

They nonetheless did not have the requisite management skills to run a government since they operated, mostly, guerilla warfare outside the colonial governance structures from which they, perhaps, would have learnt modern managerial and leadership skills ready to run a national government. Most them were no more than local chiefs and the colonialists were not keen on succession planning. This ignited a series of misrules by our founding fathers mainly due to gross leadership ignorance and thus they ended as tyrants and wreckers of economies.

Besides, many of them were torn between the West and the East due to the cold war ideologies that ran at the time which further impaired their leadership judgments leading to grave monumental blunders. Thus one may wish to forgive President Jomo Kenyatta's leadership style which was characterized by the militant approach pre-colonial era. However, one would have expected President Daniel Moi to improve the economy, human rights and legal frameworks being a second generation leader. Did this happen? President Moi's quest to consolidate power just perfected the shortcomings of founding President Kenyatta under the infamous slogan *Nyayo*, understood to mean; following in *Mzee*'s footsteps.

Kenya literally suffered under the 24 years of President Moi's leadership that lacked a clear national vision and genuine political will to empower the people. NARC's ascendancy to power early 2003 heralded Kenya's first interaction with what President Kufuor referred to as transformational leadership. Since then to-date, President Kibaki's government has been characterized by social economic development and a reversal of President Moi's poor governance. President Kibaki's test on succession leadership still hangs in the balance as we await the 2012 general elections. It is regrettable that anachronistic leaders are all over the country seeking to fill county positions both as governors and senators. It is the sincere hope of the author that the current electorate will rise above such retrogressive attitudes of electing leaders whose time has lapsed and who added no value during their hey days.

I deem it appropriate for retired leaders to mentor youthful ones to fill positions of leadership. This is the natural order even in the animal kingdom. Howbeit, power is never given, it is grabbed. Thus the youthful leadership must wage a decisive war to topple the stale leadership through sound policy, real care of the citizenry and harmonious co-existence amongst all people groups never witnessed before. There is absolutely nothing wrong with age. Age is beauty and from our African context, wisdom resides in grey hair. My argument however rests on two facts. First, most of the old guards were custodians of the repressive regime and giving then another opportunity to serve will regurgitate us to the same misdeeds of yesteryears. Secondly, in most cases, more youthful leaders are more energetic and visionary. This is why in the corporate sector, retirees are rarely re-called to be executive officers but as advisory board members.

As we seek to fill President Kibaki's huge shoes at the national platform, the country should be at the outlook for a visionary and transformational leader willing and ready to implement the new constitution to the letter. We ought to search for a leader who will negotiate real favorable trade policies between EAC and the larger markets like the EU. At the county level, only a transformational leader can set the pace and raise the bar to such high standards that the people will wonder how soon his / her term of office has lapsed. The Brazilians will forever miss their role model President Luiz Inacio Lula da Silva. His preferred heir, President Dilma Rousseff's greatest asset in Presidential campaigns was Lula's endorsement following his unprecedented development record. Those yearning for elective positions should seek to exceed the people's expectations and on this note; bravos to Peter Kenneth, the Gatanga legislator whose ground popularity is developmental based.

Lack of succession planning by leadership that clings to power for life may blame than any other parameter for the crisis witnessed in this continent and around the world. In his book, Pandemonium, Daniel Patrick Moynihan observed that it's only the U.S., Switzerland, Britain, Sweden, New Zealand, Australia, Canada and South Africa which both existed in 1914 and have not had their form of government changed by violence since then. He sees 50 new countries formed in the next 50 years due to ethnic conflict. With the secession of South Sudan from the Khartoum government early this year (2011), we have 49 to go to fulfill Moynihan's predictions.

This ethnic phenomenon is still shaping our succession leadership post the Kibaki administration. The political class in this time and age still focuses on ethnic groupings to seize power 'democratically'. Politics in our country along ethnic lines have rose to record high. Regrettably so, the 2012 elections will not be issue based but the outcome of cunningly crafted tribal amalgamations. Thus, the probability of a visionary and gifted leader hailing from a minority tribe into the comfort of State

House any time soon tends zero. President Kenyatta set a good trend by picking President Moi as his deputy for eleven years then perceived to hail from a minority Turgen group. Today however, Kalenjins have realized the power of coming together embracing their common heritage and no longer sees themselves as Nandis, Turgens, Kipsigis, Pokot and the others in the light of national politics, courtesy of President Moi's political math and the colonialists who coiled the term Kalenjin.

Reading by the signs, it is quite unlikely that President Kibaki will be neutral in the 2012 succession arrangement. It is not necessary to be neutral anyway but to unite the country; he ought not to betray his tribal clout in his preferred heir. This seems to be a serious failure amongst the so called Mt Kenya Mafia. President Moi himself beat all odds as he anointed Uhuru Kenyatta as his preferred heir dividing the Kikuyu vote in the 2002 general elections. President Kibaki's succession strategy seems to be swayed unrelenting to his golfing clique's desire to defend the status quo especially ethnic chauvinism.

This spirit is best demonstrated by the development of the KKK alliance among the Kikuyus (Uhuru Kenyatta); the Kambas (Kalonzo Musyoka) and the Kalenjins (William Ruto). Never mind that these three fellows and their cronies alike are well schooled but approaches leadership tribally merely for political survival. Prime Minister Raila went public in defense of one, Charity Ngilu, the Minister at Maji house, without even letting the due course of law to establish graft allegations leveled against her; all because of the Kamba vote block which he cannot contemplate losing. Hon Ngilu is meant to neutralize Kalonzo's influence in Ukambani in favour of Raila. By this defiant act, Raila sends one clear message: integrity can be compromised where votes are at stake and thus, naturally, I must protect my ground 'point-man' in Ukambani.

126

Undoubtedly, the domino effect guarantees that nothing will escape the political intrigues certain to pick pace. At the writing of this book, Raila, Uhuru and Kalonzo have the highest stake into acquisition of the Presidency mantle after Kibaki's reign. In my considered opinion, Saitoti and Ruto are playing second position while Martha, Mudavadi and Ngilu a distant third. Thus pointless to rate Peter Kenneth, Mwangi Kiunjuri, Eugene Wamalwa, Rev Mutava Musyimi and Bifoli Wakoli, all who have expressed interest with the top seat. Judging by our top three presidential candidates, tribal leadership that ignores integrity and fidelity will guide the apparent heir of Kibaki's official residence. Nothing based on succession planning.

In the United States, many presidents were once vice presidents. John Adams, Thomas Jefferson, Andrew Johnson, Theodore Roosevelt, Harry Truman, Richard Nixon, Lyndon Johnson, Gerald Ford and George H W Bush were all at one time vice presidents. This is not always an asset since destitute leadership can be passed on. However, grooming leaders dates back to biblical times and human history although our medieval passed on skills exclusively to their sons. Strangely enough even in our private sectors, back stabbing is more of the order than the exception rather than developing new leadership in management. Most aggressive personalities rarely find their way to the top and are perceived as potential threats to existing order.

Raila is perceived by power brokers as anti-capitalist who can easily thwart their fortunes. These fears are however unfounded and the schemer Raila is; he will undoubtedly reach out and appease all 'relevant stakeholders' in his attempt to attain the presidency. Certainly, he is a crafty and calculative go-getter. He will do anything legal within his hands to divide the Kikuyu vote. Seems like he has divided the Kamba and seems to have lost the

Kalenjin votes. Needless to point out Kalonzo's convenient raw defense of one William Ruto without respecting the ICC due process against every skill he learnt in law school. Whichever side the ball will role, it will be along tribal alignments; period! Who will rise up and slaughter this dragon: tribalism! Koigi Wamwere calls it negative ethnicity. He thought it would die after shaving his dreadlocks but the elite animal evolved to fit accurately in the 21st Century.

I wondered loudly how the Japanese handle scandals when I read of the resignation of the Justice Minister, Minoru Yanagida. His resignation was only necessitated by the fact that he jested in a public gathering that his job as Justice Minister is rather `a bit too easy'; which was seen as undermining the office he held. I don't know what it takes for our leaders to resign but perhaps if some of the economic crimes committed were done on Chinese ground, death penalty would have been executed yesterday. But do we not honestly envy these Asian Tigers and desire to be like them economically? Then we have to deeply soul search as we elect the next crop of leaders to put an end once and for all the ethnic-characterized leadership in Kenya.

Our political leaders have shamelessly appointed close relatives despite constant cries of nepotism by the civil society. President Kenyatta had a nephew and brother in law in his cabinet besides one of his daughter's becoming a mayor of Nairobi. But who could have questioned the tyranny in Kenyatta? This however is not just a Kenyan problem but a human weakness. In Africa however, nepotism has dominated succession leadership. This could be excused where absolute monarchies exist like in Swaziland. It is quite annoying when a country purports to be democratic but in the veins practices corrupted monarchy. Democracy is not perfect. Just like other forms of governance, it has its own shortcomings. Perhaps we would be more comfortable in Africa to know there are no elections rather than sham electioneering processes that abuse our intellectual capacities.

President Yoweri Kaguta Museveni of Uganda, despite having his wife Janet as a cabinet minister, just in case, has ruled since 1986 and has just been sworn in for a fourth term. After spending 24 years at the helm of power, one would have expected President Museveni to guide the likes of Besigye and Otunnu for smooth succession. Ironically, on December 15th 2010, Raila Odinga was aiding Museveni in vote hunt in Iganga district riding the same vehicle side by side – the man who has long advocated for democratic institutions! What does he stand for in succession leadership? Kalonzo Musyoka and William Ruto too visited Uganda to pledge their support to Museveni casting aspersions on their genuine conviction on reforms. The fact that President Museveni has positively turned around the Ugandan economy is unquestionable. Nevertheless, he will be well advised to prepare a fair ground for the next elections void of his candidature. This will not only secure his respect in our global village but assure him of a peaceful retirement like President Moi.

Former Soviet leader and the 1990 Nobel Peace Prize winner Michael Gorbachev marked his 80th birthday by advising Prime Minister Vladimir Putin against running for president and warning about the dangers of Arab-style social revolt. Putin and his Presidential successor Dmitry Medvedev have said on repeated occasions that they will decide in private which of them will run – and almost certainly win – in next year's elections. Gorbachev's perestroika and glasnost reforms altered the course of history by burying the Soviet Union and liberating Eastern Europe. Thus he became a free man respected worldwide with honorable retirement. Undoubtedly, had Robert Mugabe retired after two terms in office, he would now be rated slightly behind Nelson Mandela as one of the greatest leaders of his times. Now he is considered a villain by most observers at home and abroad. One can only hope that Yoweri Museveni and Paul Kagame will draw helpful lessons from history.

President George Washington, despite redeeming Americans from their British colonial masters, handed over power democratically setting the right precedence for future leaders. He didn't threaten Americans that leaders taking over power will not counter British aggression or possible internal uprisings. And since this pace was set, none of the American Presidents except Franklin Delano Roosevelt ruled for more than two terms of office. Understandably so, FDR died shortly after his fourth term of office began because of the circumstances of WW2. None of the U.S. presidents contemplates by any stretch of imagination extending his services from the Oval office beyond two terms. This is succession leadership. The result of this is that America has been for long the greatest economy and the world's only superpower with the fall of the Soviet Union.

Not far away from here, President Bingu Wa mutharika of Malawi appointed his wife Callista Nee Chapola Chimombo to cabinet and his younger brother Peter as Justice Minister. I am yet to confirm with Malawians on their unequalled gifting and outstanding credentials. On the West front of our beloved continent, President Abdoulaye Wade of Senegal is crystal clear that only his son Karim is qualified enough to succeed his seat. Again Senegalese may need to confirm these perceived qualifications or arrayed fears of a non-relative taking over power and prosecuting the past evils committed by the Wade government. Our fallen hero, President Hosni Mubarak of Egypt apparent heir was his favorite son, Gamal provoking the massive protests led by the Muslim brotherhood which compelled him to resign.

Right in our immediate neighborhood, Chama Cha Demokrasia Na Maendeleo (CHADEMA) Presidential candidate, Dr Wilbrod Slaa, claimed that the re-election of Tanzania's President, Jakaya Kikwete was the product of fabricated sham election results, and as such, CHADEMA won't recognize the results. The International Community recognizes President Kikwete who polled 61.1 per cent of the October 30th 2010 vote and sees the National Electoral Commission as a credible institution in Tanzania. But why won't Dr Slaa who garnered 26.3 per cent of the votes stop mumbo jumbo and concede as his Western counterparts have always done and help Africa move towards political maturity? What is this about hard grip to power in Africa and a crisis in succession leadership? We congratulate Hon Uhuru Kenyatta for conceding after the 2002 general elections. This led to political stability in Kenya and rejuvenation of the economy.

Guinea's Presidential elections of November 7th 2010 were disputed and the Interim President General Sekouba Konate declared a state of emergency till results were confirmed by the Supreme Court. Violence was most severe with death toll rising to seven in Ratoma, the only suburb in Conakry which defeated candidate Cellou Dalein Diallo in the votes. Alpha Conde was declared winner with 52.52 per cent of the votes against Diallo's 47.48 per cent. This was supposed to be Guinea's first democratic election after over 50 years of authoritarian rule that has led to abject poverty countrywide despite massive stores of bauxite and iron ore. Ethnic politics between the two major tribes, the Fulani and Malinke dominated the electioneering process.

Following the death of President General Lansana Conte in December 2008, General Konate was named as Defense Minister by the junta leader, Captain Moussa Dadis Camara. Gen Konate finally took over the reins of power after Capt Camara narrowly survived an assassination attempt following a protracted stalemate

131

over his intention to run for Presidency in spite of an earlier promise to the contrary. As a continent, we must congratulate the Guinean army for succession planning and in particular General Konate's leadership. He cut short his treatment in Morocco to attend the inauguration ceremony of the President elect, Prof Alpha Conde in line with the promise the army gave the Guineans to organize a civilian democratic election. We can only hope the good professor will help this nation develop its young democracy and set an unquestionable precedence of development and governance especially in smooth transition of power.

Besieged Cote d'Voire leader Laurent Gbagbo refused to hand over power to Alassane Ouattara. This is even after the Independent Electoral Commission declared Ouattara the winner of the vote on December 2nd 2010 and despite pressure amounting from ECOWAS, A.U., E.U., U.S., Canada and the U.N. Security Council. Now both leaders have claimed victory locking the already volatile nation into a possible bloody stand-off. The 65 year old incumbent occupies the presidential palace and his ministers appear to exercise control over their departments, while Ouattara is trying to control the levels of the state from a hotel protected by U.N. peace keepers. By Friday the 17th Dec 2010, nine people had been shot dead even as ICC warns it will charge suspects.

In a country that has seen several bouts of violence during a decade-long political crisis, the deadlock is a volatile cocktail, and General Gbagbo's generals led by Army Chief of Staff General Philippe Mangou have issued a stark warning to international troops. In 2002 a failed putsch against Gbagbo plunged Cote d'Voire into a conflict that split the country between the rebel mainly-Muslim north and Gbagbo's richer Christian south. One would have expected President Gbagbo's experience then to motivate him to relinquish power after his two terms in office peacefully and honorary rather than leave Ivoirians flabbergasted.

In a twist of events, the African Union responded promptly and rejected any attempt to create a *fait accompli* that undermines the Cote d''Ivoire's electoral process. Obviously, Gbagbo who garnered 45.9% of the votes against Ouattara's 51% wants to blackmail the country into a power sharing deal. Coincidentally, its former South African President, Thabo Mbeki who was initially commissioned by the E.U. to broker a political deal as he did in Zimbabwe where incumbent Robert Mugabe lost to Tsvangirai with 43% against the latter's 47% of the popular vote. Mbeki's effort didn't arrive at the desired results and the AU chairman, Jean Ping was then commissioned to lead the attempt in breaking the stalemate. Many other leaders have attempted to mediate in the Ivorian crisis including Prime Minister Raila Odinga with little success at the writing of this book. This seems to be the new face of Africa's *coup d'etata* which we hope will not recur in Kenya from unsatisfied electoral losers who just cannot concede.

In the Democratic Republic of Congo, individual warlords operate mines and run their own police forces to enforce their control – a legacy they inherited from their father Mobutu Sese Seko. Interestingly, President Joseph Kabila jetted in Kenya on March 4th 2011 in person pleading with his counterpart President Kibaki to assist him in his treasure search for his lost 2.5 tonne gold worth Ksh 8.5billion. The narco-states of West Africa like Guinea Bissau, the value of cocaine trafficked through its ports is higher than its GDP. Such leadership may not willingly prepare for succession which is likely to scuttle their multi-billion dollar black market trade. May be that's the reason the ICC is now freezing the vast wealth accumulated by African warlords after their arrest as is the case of Charles Taylor, former Liberian strong man whose hard grip on power was earmarked by blood diamonds and weakened by a beauty model.

William Kabogo who won the Juja by-elections following the court's nullification of George Thuo's 2007 election claimed throughout the campaign period that the latter was using the projects that he had initiated during his tenure to woo voters. The question before us: Was Thuo supposed to ignore and trash his predecessor's projects? Isn't this retrogressive politics? Could this cheap propagandist deceit have caused Thuo his parliamentary seat? I wish I could know the advice that the spunky Martha Karua, the 'father-head' of the aptly nick-named flower party that was Kabogo's and Kioko Mbuvi's SPV gives her mentees on developmental continuity. I also wonder whether if Kabogo were elected the President whether he would crash the proposed Lamu port and the two railway lines connecting Lamu – Juba and Nairobi – Addis Ababa so that glory doesn't go to the outgoing Kibaki Presidency.

In a landmark ruling by a Nyahururu court, the Ol Kalou member of parliament, Erastus Mureithi, was ordered to complete a community project started by his predecessor, Muriuki Karue, through government's devolved funds or risk a six month civil jail term in contempt. Mr Erastus Mureithi had ignored the completion of a dispensary building worth Kshs 6.5 Million fearing that it might give Muriuki Karue some political mileage. Never mind that Erastus Mureithi is a well educated chap and a former high flying banker. Did Hon Mureithi ignore the strategic goals that his predecessor at Cooperative bank had formulated as he took over the office of the chief executive? Is this the style of leadership we anticipate for our Counties? Projects ran for political gains? Thanks to senior magistrate Alice Mong'are who understands and safeguards the vitality of succession leadership as she made that momentous ruling for the sake of a desperately needy public.

Hon Kabogo's and Mureithi's cases are not unique but just a representative of the shape of politics in Kenya. We the people then must reform the attitudes of our leaders. The cost of vacuum in leadership is too dear to dare it. We must seek to be guided by principled policies rather than cheap politicking that take advantage of the ignorant masses. Since the political elite know that professionals have no time to educate their people, they take advantage and appeal to the not-so-schooled crowds. I am sending a challenge to all professionals to wake up to this call and go back to their constituents and enlighten them. Time and gain, politicians say that their game is about numbers – most numbers have low capacity and can be lured through cash and eloquence of empty rhetoric.

On 2nd March 2011, Cooperative and Marketing minister, Hon Joseph Nyagah appointed Dr Daniel Langat as the new managing director of New Kenya Cooperative Creameries. That seat had been absent since 30th November 2009 when he refused to renew the term of then MD Francis Mwangi for unclear reasons. I am amazed that a performing MD's term failed to be renewed with vague excuses to this very day. It is more interesting that the allegations rallied against him in parliament were wanting but none of the legislators was willing to vehemently fight for the good course not only for Mr Mwangi but more importantly for the dairy industry he helped to get back on track. Do you invite a performing MD for an interview as Mr Nyagah attempted or carry an appraisal on his performance? The NewKCC case is the best indicator of a broken succession planning system whereby appointments are intuition based disrespecting a plainly laid down criterion. Why fix it if it is working – and within the legally stipulated number of terms of office? At age 70, the micro finance pioneer and the 2006 Nobel Peace Prize winner, Muhammad Yunus still led Grameen bank with alertness of mind and unequalled creativity and innovation.

For political leadership positions, succession planning can be a complex subject. However, for the County Executives and other employees for the county government, succession planning can be organized from the same principles that guide other organizations, profit or none profit making. Succession planning is a part of the process of preparing for the future of an organization in anticipation for change. Every key position and key person in an organization is a candidate for a succession plan. The important impact is that it is virtually impossible to successfully promote someone unless there is a trained person to take over the position being vacated. It is Lady Nancy Astor who observed, "The main dangers in this life are the people who want to change everything or nothing".

The key challenges in succession planning are the diversity of workplaces and employees due to globalization; skyrocketed business environment complexity; elimination of middle level management thus reducing considerable grooming time; large gaps between one job level and the next one above it; increased hopping of employees from one employer to another and organizations that always promote and develop existing employees can become non innovative, traditional and redundant. Hiring from outside can bring in new technologies not available inside, as well as new ideas and ways of doing things. But the down side is that acquiring new talent can be extremely expensive.

To effectively implement a succession plan, the county leadership may need to consider the long-term direction they want to give the county through an effective strategic plan guiding organizational course and direction; the key areas which require continuity and development of the people resources within the county; the key people the county wants to develop and nurture for the future; the concept of succession planning in the light of the county strategies like concentrating efforts in the areas where the returns will be highest; the career paths that the county's most talented people should be following. Each path should be customized to fit the abilities and talents of the people involved. Succession plans should make opportunities for each individual as they grow and mature, so that the county can keep them challenged and stimulated, and not lose them to other, possibly faster moving organizations. The plans should be proactive, with people moving into different areas for experience and training before they are needed in critical positions, rather than reactive - waiting for openings to occur, then scurrying around to find an appropriate candidate at the last second.

Some of the strategies that a county government should consider for succession planning process are recognize that there are different approaches which may be used, depending on the situation per department; the county can move some people along quickly, in order to expose them to a broad range of experiences, and possibly to fill vacancies; a deeper involvement in selected departments or disciplines may be indicated; culture and processes that the county desires to develop; individual's capabilities and competencies; structure and operations of the county; the capabilities and strengths of the people who currently occupy the key positions in the municipal and county councils within the county government's jurisdictions, and how they will be positioned in the light of devolved government; a succession plan for key areas of responsibility in the county that should be reviewed at least once a year.

The main advantages of succession planning are perpetual supply of well trained, broadly experienced, well-motivated people who are ready and able to step into key positions as needed; a cadre of desirable candidates who are being integrated into the county management with positive goals established for them individually; a flow of these capable people through various departments with the goals of educating them into the culture and processes of the county; alignment of the future needs of the county with the availability of appropriate resources within the county; positive goals for key personnel, which will help keep them within the county and will help assure the continuing supply of capable successors for each of the important positions included in the succession plan; defined career paths, which will help the county recruit and retain better people; continuous input of ideas to improve the internal processes and procedures of the county, as well as the opportunities to improve the offerings and services of the county in the marketplace; by going internal, counties will save money, enhance employee engagement and morale, and gain ample time to get to know promotion candidates quite well; and succession planning will help the county government in evaluating whether the goals are results-oriented focused on the desired county culture.

Therefore, I will work, I will save, I will sacrifice, I will endure; I will fight cheerfully, and do my utmost, as if the issue of the whole struggle depended on me alone - Martin Treptow

Setting County Systems Right

In Malcolm Gladwell's book, The Tipping Point, the author candidly addresses how little things can make a big difference. Commenting on the Theory of the Broken Windows which was the brain child of criminologists James Wilson and George Kelling, they argued that crime was the inevitable result of disorder. Thus, if a window is broken and left unrepaired, passersby will conclude that no one cares and hence no one is in charge. Soon, more windows will be broken, and the sense of anarchy will spread from the building to the street it faces, sending the signal that anything goes. Buglers, muggers, robbers and rapists believe that they reduce their chances of being arrested if they operate in places where potential victims are already intimidated by the prevailing conditions.

On the same antidote, unless systems are set right in the first place, the new constitutional order is open for abuse. No government schemes can perfect men / women. Laws are subjective in nature rather than objective and thus meaning is only attained through their application to serve humanity. Mortals cannot be perfect and thus the real test is not in setting systems right but a change of attitude from greed to servitude. Otherwise a cruel leadership can assume *carte blanche* and restructure the intent of this new found constitutional hope which is robbing the 6th Babylonian 1st dynasty King Hammurabi the law giver his place in shaping the society structurally through his code. It is Nelson Mandela who once said, "Sometimes it falls upon a generation to be great. You can be that generation." We are well able to be that generation that will stand up and set the devolved governance systems right and seek to follow their stipulations from the very onset.

Nevertheless, we ought to and must set the systems. Man is corrupt by nature. Period. It has been said and of a fact that you can't truly know a thief unless and until you give them a chance. Our disdain nature is corrupt and we all agree that power corrupts and absolute power corrupts absolutely. It is for this reason that we began the search for a constitution that seals corrupt loopholes. But the constitution is a blue print. Besides enacting several laws to compliment the new found constitution, we must also put in place working systems that will guide the nitty gritties of running the new constitutional order, more so at the county level. It takes lots of energies and considerable amount of time to fix systems but we must never tire.

The United States Constitution was drafted by Jacob Shallus in 1787 under the watch of George Washington. It greatly violated human rights as we know them today. First, it allowed slavery and had clauses that permitted the state to punish any escaping slave and barred any law that illegalized slavery. Besides, it barred women and black Americans from voting. However, the 13th, 15th and 19th amendments changed all these outdated laws since the U.S leadership adapted to a system of governance that serves the current needs of its citizenry. I really don't intend to keep waving the U.S. flag but must nevertheless acknowledge that that great country has had good leaders, at least to the American people themselves, all other debates aside.

By and large, the success of the United States has had to do with fast tracking the reform process that is issue based rather than personalities' centered. Thus, in the U.S. federal system of governance, the `who' is in power is not as important as the policies he is bound to follow. The systems are so crystal clear that even the so called `Son of Kenya' President cannot favor his father's homeland at the expense of his nation's policies. But can we rise to this level of governance? Yes, by doing it right in the first place.

In my considered opinion, just like a competitive organization, at least the county governments should have minimally the following systems for a start for effective functioning:

- Customer Service system
- Procurement system
- Finance system
- Project Management system
- Human Resource system

- Infrastructural System
- Information Technology System
- Natural Resources Management System

Customer Service System

For leadership to reach the highest plausible success point, it must be accountable and responsive to its customers. It must be customer oriented rather than leaders' focused. It's about the people being served and not who is serving. It's about service delivery. A customer service system should incorporate a deliberate and conscious effort to reach to customers. As such, a customer satisfaction baseline survey ought to be established from the outset. This then must be followed by periodic checks and regular situational analysis. Suggestions, compliments and complaints 'boxes' from customers are necessary but not sufficient. The current public system has all this but few, if any, really care on the contents whereof.

Recently I was engaged to offer consultancy services to a public sector organization. It took nine months for payments to come through and after lots of follow up. Sadly, this being a parastatal, I expected services to be more efficient that mainstream ministries. I had none to run to for payments to be made since our courts take longer to determine outcome. As an external customer, I needed a clear arbitration; not a kangaroo court. I needed payments, not stories. My story is not unique. Many other suppliers of goods and services to this authority complained equally about delayed payments. Neither is the story unique about the organization in question but the entire public sector. The county leadership ought to deviate from this current 'process' based system of governance to 'results' based governance system.

I am cognizant of the government reform system popularly known as performance contracting. For this progress, I tell the current government: Bravos! Encore! The reality on the ground to customers is a different episode altogether. I look forward to county governments that will treat customers with the same spirit, or even more, that the private sector in handling clients. Once an employee fails the customer service system, the private sector doesn't constitute an investigation committee. The responsible culprit leaves sooner than she was hired and the organization moves forward. This is not brutality but efficiency. It's focusing on the service and not the individual. County leaders must appreciate that the focus are the thousands of stakeholders that they sought to serve as they solicited for their trust through the ballot box. In business we say, the customer is always right. In the U.S., customer is the king and in Japan, customer is the god. Sounds extreme. The message is simple, all intents, policies, focus and other county systems must be customer oriented.

Procurement System
The biggest buyer in any country is the government; a truth that anyone in her right frame of mind knows. The greatest gulf between the 'halves' and the 'halve nots' is pegged on one's inclination to the public procurement system. Being politically correct, if you like. The concept of direct relationship between success and hard work borders hypocrisy – let's face it, Kenyans. The so called 'competitive bidding' is an insult to our intelligence. We have a system of governance where the tender winner is predetermined long before the procurement process begins. At extreme cases, a *tenderer* is even asked to submit all the required proposals while ensuring the company that she wishes to win quotes the lowest bid.

Beginners in public tenders religiously continue to tender faithfully believing competitive bidding is taking place. They then think they lost the tender fairly and only hope that some-day the gods will be on their side. At the meantime, a sacred cow wins a multi-billion tender, say, supply of electronic voting registers, and since he is in good records with his bankers, financing is availed. Profits in the realm of billions rake into his account in a single deal and he spends the rest of his time politicking and golfing while his supposedly tendering competitors continue sweating for survival. With more cash at disposal, he can now buy the one who calls the shots for future deals of similar or bigger magnitude. And the cycle continues year in year out.

Ironically, the current public procurement system as guided by the PPOA is a rigorous process supposedly tight lipped system with enough stages of checks and balances. But has it worked? Should this be devolved to the county governments, we shall only devolve corruption and impoverish the country all the more as we attempt to enrich an already expansive and expensive system. Professionals who have studied supply chain and have been in practice understand all the bottle necks and are familiar with all the existing loopholes. But do they have the goodwill to enhance the establishment of a corrupt free procurement system as we constitute the county governments?

In my opinion, a joint effort between the existing government authorities like PPOA and KACC ought to pull their human resources together with the private sector to assist in the development of a procurement system that will nurture entrepreneurship at the grassroots. Then and only then shall the country move forward. Capitalism as practiced in Kenya has many pros but equally numerous cons. For instance, the Ministry of roads demands that any prospective contactor must show case evidence of previous works done prior to registration with the ministry. But when did this contractor execute works before registration. The pretence from the ministry officials in charge is

145

that one ought to have done *small* works with the local government or private developers. But again heavy machinery is required before registration. How do you buy machines before you are even registered? Consequently, we have to keep hiring Chinese companies since we discourage developing local entrepreneurs. Moreover, in the example of road works, contractors will undergo rigorous prequalification procedures with KeRRA, KURA and KENHA annually and roughly 95% will not get any works even after the prequalification while 5% get all the works. Are there two levels of pre-qualifications?

This scenario cuts across all the ministries. Will our county governments rise up to the occasion and encourage thousands to do business with the government? Yes, through an intelligent procurement system that awards tenders on preset conditions. For instance, the system, IT based, could ensure that no one gets a contract before all who prequalified get. Or at least enhance that every prequalified supplier of goods and services gets a certain amount of work (value-wise) before anyone gets round two. This system could also incorporate multiple realities like youth, gender and people living with disabilities as well as geographical location of constituents to enhance equitable distribution of works. We honestly cannot continue doing the same things in the same manner and expect different results. This is madness.

The procurement systems must be fixed by men and women with goodwill if the Kenyan dream will ever be achieved. If *wananchi* were vigilant in ensuring the procurement system as it is today is followed as outlined by the PPOA act, transparency would be achieved. But Kenyans fear victimization and at the end all the commoners suffer. The criterion for evaluating technical proposals is clear and results should be disclosed prior to opening the financial proposals. This almost never happens as supply chain officers take advantage of either the cowardice or/and

146

ignorance of the tenders participants. Moreover, financials should be opened and the tender amounts read loudly in the presence of all tendering entities. We must be vigilant to set out the right traditions at the county levels before they get corrupted by historical injustices.

Finance System
The county governments must set the finance systems right from revenue collection to expenditure including priority lines. Finances are the engine that drives organizations. This system ought to be so transparent as to allow the constituents to query all expenditure during the AGMs or open days, whatever they call them. Truly, the Country Assemblies will put the County Executives into continuous checks. But they can all be bought into silence. The finance system should be open to public scrutiny just like the public liability companies will publish their audited accounts.

I understand that the Nairobi Chapel is the fastest growing church in East Africa at the writing of this book. There could be a lot of explanations to this growth pattern but one fundamental factor is the transparent manner in which they keep their account books. All parishioners can view the church's audited accounts. This makes them feel confident with their shepherds. Similarly, county governments should be able to publish their accounts books through a locally operated county journal as well as an interactive website for customers' contributions. All tenders awarded should be made public. This is public matter and public expenditure should be published.

The constitution must ride higher than any other written law. The idea of stealing money in the military reigns and refuse to account for fraudulent deals in the disguise of state secrets is an insult to the right to information inscribed in our constitution. It is such

147

broken systems that have permitted drug money laundering and siphoning public funds off shore. Both at the national and county levels, the devolved government must develop a system that protects the economy from piracy, laundering and siphoning money to foreign accounts. Fraudulently acquired monies finding their way into our economy may explain the phenomenal skyrocketing prices in the urban real estate depriving many families the hope of ever having a town home. If every county is on the watch, development will be devolved to the people.

Project Management System
Sacred cow projects in Kenya have been the norm in previous regimes rather than the exception. At this time and age, no single project should ever be implemented on the sentiments or mere feelings of a county leader. Project Management is a discipline that helps to logically implement projects within predetermined objectives of scope, cost and time to meet all stakeholders' expectations. County governments will be encountered with many important projects that ought to be implemented. In times past, projects in Kenya have been implemented to satisfy political causes. As such, a project may not necessarily be a critical activity but as long as it will be used by the political leader for the next election's leverage, then it is given preeminence.

I wonder what the county aspirants are planning beyond the election day; or are they arguing we will know when we cross the bridge. There are modern ways of prioritizing projects; numeric and non numeric methods. Since this is not a project management manual, the writer will not get into these laborious details. Of importance is to implement projects based on a rational and scientific project management approach. This will call for all stakeholder involvement under the able guidance of professionals in relevant fields. If you were to run a county government with obviously limited resources, what would you prioritize between:

security, health, education, water availability, agriculture, entrepreneurship, roads networks, electricity and floods mitigation? Why? Which part of the county? This calls for a project management system as discussed in greater details elsewhere in this book.

In a workable project management system; the competitive advantage, comparative advantage and cost benefit analysis of the project must be considered without ignoring all other subjective realities in the county. The system should guide the implementers on the net present value of each project as viewed by the market at its completion. This would help counties to compete in a healthy manner in moving Kenya forward. Just like a family, governments must have priorities and guidelines on implementing projects that will propel the counties to operate as profitable organizations in the 21st Century. Again no need of inventing the wheel. Project Management Systems have been tested and found working. All our county governments need is to benchmark – creatively and innovatively adapt them for their unique settings through professional guidance.

Human Resource System
Someone observed: we use up nature's natural resources but using them up, and we use up man's natural resources by not using them up at all. This is tragic at best. We waste gifted brains in an attempt to appease our cronies or strategically position bed fellows who will 'cooperate' in siphoning the public coffers 'wisely'. Hon Henry Kosgey ignored the names forwarded by the board in appointing one, John Koskey to head NEMA. Clearly, the honorable Minister still has the old notion of rewarding people though lucrative jobs. An idea whose time has passed is sick at best, Mr honorable! This has characterized Kenya's' leadership system, it stoops that low. I have no doubt that the Minister's choice, Mr Kokgey, is qualified for the prestigious job, but how

149

did the honorable minister manage to ignore the existing outlined procedure? Aren't we bound to repeat this same historical arrogance? How different will our counties behave?

I must caution my readers that Hon Koskey's illustration is by no means unique but just picked as a case study to extrapolate on the vitality of enhancing that a workable Human Resource System is set in place in our county governments. To refresh your memory, Hon Amos Kimunya while acting as minister of transport named Stephen M. Gichuki as the Kenya Airports Authority boss ignoring all expert advice. Similarly, Prof Anyang' Nyong'o ignored all protocol in appointing Dr. Olang'o Onundi as director of the Kenya Medical Training College. I have no idea how the President appointed Ndegwa Muhoro as the new CID director on the eve of the new constitution's promulgation; much less how the Prime Minister's younger sister became Kenya's consul-general in Los Angeles, USA. The list is endless. But all these appointments seem to take a tribal connotation so strong as to ignore professional recruitment procedures.

I am yet to understand the criteria in which Ambassadors are picked in this country. No idea about the magic used but I can make a not-too-foolish guess: connections with the political elite. Since it is hard to teach an old dog new tricks, we have an opportunity as Kenyans to demand a HR system in our respective counties before vacancies are filled up clan-wise. I suggest that a HR system that allows the scrutiny by all county constituents ought to be developed. Such a system should allow the public purportedly being served by this Human Resource to understand the recruitment, retention and exit platform of every county employee.

We have suffered brain drain far too long. A transparent, credible and people based HR system will attract professionals from across the Diaspora back home. If each citizen concentrated with what they can do best, the only feasible option is to move forward. No resource precedes the human resource. If our county governments can attract, retain and motivate its work force as well as respect professional decisions void of political interferences, our country will witness growth rates never scaled before in human history. The emphasis here is to recruit people based on their capabilities, qualifications, experiences, ingenuity and all it takes to convince the county constituents that the HR system is merit based. It is people who work and not systems, policies and guidelines. Getting the right people for the right job can only translate into county success. Thus the whole idea about getting the right work force must start and remain above board.

Infrastructural System
It will be interesting for the electorate to find out the infrastructural agenda of the aspirants to public offices. Do they envision a water engineering, road engineering, housing engineering, electricity engineering, and telecommunications department as one whole or separate entities? Or are they seeking ways and means of consolidating a single efficient county infrastructural system with distinct subsets? Will the infrastructural systems compromise environmental conditions or enhance? It is much easier to address these queries if the county leadership perceives infrastructure as a whole comprising of various interlocking and interdependent parts.

I cannot promise to offer an outright solution to such a complex situation. But consider what conventionally goes on in our urban settings. When a road is under construction, the water, sewer and electric systems are interfered with. We occasionally experience sewer breakdowns in various parts of the country as recently witnessed in Naivasha besides a number of estates in Nairobi especially during road works. Moreover, garbage disposal in our major cities has become a menace at best. The contractors of the three lots of the Nairobi-Thika super-high-way have blamed delays to completing the project in time on other infrastructural works especially electricity and water besides heavy traffic controls.

Personally I envision all the infrastructural works as a major whole comprising of various sub sets rather than distinct and independent systems. Under such an arrangement, a county has an infrastructural head who chairs the various sections of endeavor. This will help the engineer in charge of cable networks, water, roads, electricity, sewer and garbage management factor in the inter-relationships between their various sections and how they influence the whole. Thus under this model, as a road is being constructed, the internet connectivity and all other systems are taken into place during the road design work. The same will be taken into consideration for all other infrastructural works in the county. Our young vibrant professionals are well capable to assist the leadership in designing an infrastructural system that not only incorporates all the works hitherto; but also assists in decision making in regard to lines of priorities, allocations of finances, monitoring progress and advising on expansion among other vitalities.

Information Technology System
To me, all other systems will be developed, designed, maintained and continually improved by a modern information technology system. The world has turned many times since the discovery and use of computers. The power of computers has revolutionalized our banking, health, service, manufacturing, management, military, transport, education, tourism and communications industry. The government has undertaken an ambitious `computer villages' project countrywide and a computer city near Machakos has been proposed – efforts worth praising.

The IT system as advanced by the author is a system that supports all other systems that a county government will be running. The system above all will assist in proper record keeping and the smooth running of accounts, finance, procurement, HR, infrastructural, M&E, customer service and project management systems among many others. Moreover, counties need an IT system that allows interconnectivity among all county branch offices as well as across all functional units. This will dramatically enhance information exchange. To this end, networking and data management professionals must be hired to meet the desired needs of a county IT system.

As such, the County Executive must of necessity start right by developing and adopting a tailor made efficient IT system. We have wasted tremendous time in the past tracing very important files at Sheria house, Nyayo house, Ardhi house and Maji house among several government offices simply because searching for the hard copies for an entire country has never been a cat walk. We can avoid creating this problem by learning from our past misdeeds and being solution conscious. We must never go back. The way out is to be organized at the very start before countless of papers start to pile up into irresolvable stocks. That's why we must hire professionals who can set the systems with the assistance of outsourced consultancy services. It is much costlier to try to clean up the desks later on.

I hope that the central government will come up with ways and means of monitoring progress of the county governments without undue interference that lags development. Right now, an IT system should be underway that will connect all the counties, the funding they anticipate from the Treasury and the projects intended to be implemented in any given fiscal year. Such an It system should monitor the progress of budgeted projects and help

153

advice for further funding. A leaf could be borrowed from the current CDF system that guides constituency funding. However, the counties are larger and the budgets bigger necessitating the need for a more comprehensive system that can support large data bases. County governments nonetheless ought not to wait for supervision from Nairobi.

Natural Resources Management System
An inevitable system that must be set right in all counties is the natural resources management plan. For instance, Lake Naivasha's waters have fallen by four meters in recent past causing riparian life to disappear at alarming rates. Conservation measures targeting degradation of forests by the lake side, human-wildlife conflict, pollution and floricultural commercial activities relying on the lake waters. In a November 2010 meeting, Prof Hiroyuki Hino, an economic expert, said solutions to the problem include afforestation of catchments, reclamation of the riparian land and re-designing Naivasha town and its vicinity to provide basic facilities and infrastructure.

Britain's Prince Charles also offered a hand of assistance to restore the Lake's former glory. The population of this town has risen from 40,000 to 500,000 without corresponding increase in services like the breakdown of the sewer system. What is true for Naivasha is true for many urban centers in Kenya like Lamu. On this particular note, we must congratulate the Prime Minister, Raila Odinga for his relentless fight to save the Mau, Lake Naivasha and other natural resources ignoring political hoi poloi and obviously taking his much envied political career though an acid litmus test – this is leadership. Our heroine in the campaign in conservation of natural resources, Prof Wangari Mathai, will go down memory lane as an astute woman who saved the place of habitat for our children's children.

It is imperative for the county leadership to set the management of the natural resources system from the outset in the light of the evolving debate on climate change. In this case, anyone who falls in the wrong hands of the law governing management of natural resources will not cry foul. Similarly, provision of basic amenities ought to be planned way into the future factoring in population trends among various other dynamics. It's very regrettable, to say the least, to witness breakdown of sewer systems and garbage rotting within human residence. Observably so, most municipal councils inherited this crisis from previous managements. But how long shall we blame the misdeeds of our former leaders? And what shall the next generation say of us after the torch of responsibility was passed on?

The crux of the matter is that we must arise and set the systems from the word go with the inauguration of the county governments. Environmentalists ought to advice the much needed balance between the merits and demerits derived from economic activities that threaten the sustainability of natural resources in the formulation of a natural resources management system. With such a system, floricultural firms around Lake Naivasha and elsewhere will do business through stipulated natural resources guidelines and policies devoid of either malice or favoritism. Efforts are at high gear to conserve rain water countrywide and one such a dam has been opened in Machakos. County governments should follow suit among various other creative ways to conserve water catchments.

Other Systems
The county governments must also set a disaster management system within their jurisdictions. The floods witnessed in Bundalang'i, the droughts experienced in northern Kenya, the fire outbursts all over as was the tragic incident of Nakumatt Supermarket in the city center, the terrorists' bomb blasts and

sports grounds stampede like the Nyayo stadium incident ought not to rob us our beloved citizens. The fire extinguishers from our city fathers are nothing but a sham. The incoming county governments could borrow a leaf from the concerted rescue of the 33 miners trapped about 500 meters in the earth's crust in Chile. The U.S. volcanic coastline and Japan are hit by frequent cyclones. The northern parts of our globe have snowy stricken winters but their citizens are relaxed due to the confidence they have on their authorities' preparedness for eventualities. We too should set up clear policies to effectively coordinate our response to disasters both at county and national levels.

This chapter cannot exhaust all the systems that a county government need to develop. In addition to the systems discussed above, any objective county government should also seek to develop a communications, planning, accounts, monitoring an evaluation and growth and development system among many more as deemed appropriate. The intent of the author in this chapter is to show case the necessity of developing systems right from outset. Getting things right in the first place rather than a fire fighting rescue management approach. It has been said and of a fact that failure to plan implies planning to fail. Every county leadership should develop a clear on-ground practical strategic plan through a consultative process from all key stakeholders.

Such a plan should not be meant to decorate the shelves or make impressions especially to prospective development partners. A strategic plan should be a genuine blue print that guides the county development and it is followed to the letter. This document will be supported by the systems discussed above and detailed work plans with clear timeframes and persons responsible. Systems direct action. They are not an end on their own. It is people who implement these good actions rather than well devised intelligent systems. Hence the need to have the right leadership from the word go. A corrupt leadership will have means of circumventing any humanly developed system, no matter how complex and thorough.

Nevertheless, we can't look down upon working systems. It is much worse to run a `system-less' system! It is more prone to corruption and deceit. At least working systems minimize corrupt dealers and their existence alone makes the despond think twice. I plead with my country women and men that we actively get involved in the affairs of the respective counties from which we originate. We can no longer keep off and expect a minority few to remain focused and accountable. Leadership must feel the led. Then and only then will any good system work for our general good in our quest to eradicate poverty, illiteracy and disease from our soil. If we rise up to this sacred occasion, we can finally join our brothers and sisters from our global village in proclaiming that the government of the people by the people will never vanish from the face of the earth.

God bless Kenya! God bless Kenya! God bless Kenya!

References

Buch, Esteban. Beethoven's Ninth: A Political History. Chicago: University of Chicago, 2003

Clyde Sanger, Malcolm MacDonald: Bringing an end to Empire, 1995

Dambisa Moyo, Dead Aid, 2009

Daniel Patrick Moynihan, Pandemonium: Ethnicity in International Politics, 3rd March1994

Gerry Loughran, Birth of a Nation, 2010

Heilbroner, Robert L. The Nature and Logic of Capitalism. New York: W. W. Norton & Company, 1985

John Agyekum Kufuor, Development priorities for Africa, 2010

Kang, YouYoung. "Singing the Republic." Scripps College, Claremont, 29 Sept. 2004

Malcolm Gladwell, The Tipping Point: How little things can make a big difference, 7th January 2002

Malcolm MacDonald, Titans and Others, 1972

Michela Wrong, It's our turn to eat, 19th February 2009

Murithi Mutiga, Sunday Nation Publication, 8th August 2010

Paulo Freire, Pedagogy of the Oppressed, 1970

Rebecca Luhn Wolfe, Systematic Succession Planning: Building Leadership from Within, 2004

Renan, Ernest. "What Is a Nation?" Nation and Narration. Ed. Homi K. Bhabha. London: Routledge, 1990

Richard P. Appelbaum, Theories of Social Change: Markham Publishing Company Chicago, 1970.

William J. Rothwell, Effective Succession Planning: Ensuring Leadership Continuity and Building Talent From Within, 30th May 2005

Sites Visited

en.wikipedia.org/wiki/Jacob_Shallus

http://ancienthistory.about.com/b/2007/10/06/hammurabi.htm

http://atheism.about.com/library/glossary/general/bldef_hammura
bi.htm

http://www.archives.gov/exhibits/charters/constitution

http://www.britannica.com/EBchecked/topic/111803/China

http://www.gov.cn/english/laws/2005-09/19/content_64906.htm.

http://www.state.gov/r/pa/ei/bgn/18902.htm

www.indystar.com

www.planning.nsw.gov.au

www.processimpact.com

APPENDICES

APPENDIX 1: Constituencies per Province

North Eastern	Rift Valley	Western
Fafi	Baringo Central	Bungoma Central
Garisa	Baringo North	Bungoma East
Ijara	Bomet	Bungoma North
Lagdera	Bureti	Bungoma South
Mandera Central	East Pokot	Bungoma West
Mandera East	Eldoret East	Bunyula
Mandera North	Eldoret West	Busia
Mandera West	Kajiado North	Butere
Wajir East	Kajiado South	Emuhaya
Wajir North	Keiyo	Hamisi
Wajir South	Kericho	Kakamega Central (Lurambi)
Wajir West	Kipkelion	Kakamega East (Shinyalu)
	Koibatek	Kakamega North (Malava)
Eastern	Kwanza	Kakamega South (Ikolomani)
Buuri	Laikipia East	Lugari
Embu East	Laikipia North	Mt Elgon
Embu West	Laikipia South	Mumias
Garbatula	Laikipia West	Samia
Igembe South	Loima	Teso North
Imenti North	Loitoktok	Teso South
Imenti South	Marakwet	Vihiga

Isiolo	Marigat	
Kagundo	Mogotio	**Nyanza**
Kathiani	Molo	Bondo
Kathonzweni	Naivasha	Borabu
Kibwezi	Nakuru	Gucha
Kilungu	Nakuru North	Homa Bay
Kitui Central	Nandi Central	Anyanya
Kitui West	Nandi East	Kisii Central
Kyuso	Nandi North	Kisii South
Maara	Nandi South	Kisumu East
Machakos	Narok North	Kisumu West
Makueni	Narok South	Kuria East
Marsabit North	Njoro	Kuria West
Marsabit South	North Pokot	Manga
Masinga	Nyahururu	Marani
Matungulu	Pokot Central	Masaba
Mbeere North	Samburu Central	Mbita
Mbeere South	Samburu East	Migori
Mbooni East	Samburu North	Ndhiwa
Mbooni West	Sotik	North Masaba
Meru Central	Tinderet	Nyakach
Meru South	Trans Nzoia East	Nyamache
Moyale	Trans Nzoia West	Nyamira
Mukaa	Transmara	Nyamira North
Mutitu	Turkana Central	Nyando
Mutomo	Turkana East	Nyatike
Mwala	Turkana North	Rachuonyo North
Mwingi	Turkana South	Rachuonyo South
Nzaui	Turkana West	Rarienda
Tharaka North	Wareng	Rongo
Tharaka South	West Pokot	Siaya
Tigania East		South Gucha
Tigania West	**Nairobi**	Suba

Yatta	Nairobi East	Uriri
	Nairobi North	
	Nairobi West	
	Westlands	

Central		
Gatanga	Kipipiri	Nyandarua North
Gatundu	Kirinyaga Central	Nyandarua South
Githunguri	Kirinyaga East	Nyandarua West
Kabete	Kirinyaga South	Nyeri Central
Kandara	Kirinyaga West	Nyeri East
Kiambaa	Lari	Nyeri South
Kiambu East	Mirangini	Ruiru
Kiambu West	Mukurweini	Thika East
Kieni West	Murang'a East	Thika West
Kieni East	Murang'a South	
Kigumo	Nyandarua Central	

APPENDIX 2: The 47 Counties of Kenya

1. Mombasa
2. Kwale
3. Kilifi
4. Tana River
5. Lamu
6. Taita Taveta
7. Garissa
8. Wajir
9. Mandera
10. Marsabit
11. Isiolo
12. Meru
13. Tharaka Nithi
14. Embu
15. Kitui
16. Machakos
17. Makueni
18. Nyandarua
19. Nyeri
20. Kirinyaga
21. Murang'a
22. Kiambu
23. Turkana
24. West Pokot
25. Samburu
26. Trans Nzoia
27. Uasin Gishu
28. Elgeyo/Marakwet
29. Nandi
30. Baringo
31. Laikipia
32. Nakuru
33. Narok
34. Kajiado
35. Kericho
36. Bomet
37. Kakamega
38. Vihiga
39. Bung'oma
40. Busia
41. Siaya
42. Kisumu
43. Homa Bay
44. Migori
45. Kisii
46. Nyamira
47. Nairobi City

ABOUT THE AUTHOR

Kinyanjui Nganga is pursuing his PhD in the University of Nairobi in Project Planning and Management. He holds a Master of Arts degree in Project Planning and Management from the University of Nairobi and a Bachelor of Science degree in Mathematics and Physics from Jomo Kenyatta University of Agriculture and Technology.

Kinyanjui is a classified orator and an outstanding motivational speaker. He is the director of *Shape Afrika*, a private limited liability company in organizational research, Project Management and training besides lecturing in Project Management in various Universities.

Kinyanjui is happily married to *Mercy Nganga*, an IT Consultant and they have been blessed with one daughter, *Ivy* and one son, *Zig*. They reside in Nairobi – Kenya.

Kinyanjui has also published: *The Power of the Spoken Word*, *Ultimate Success* and *No More Prophets*.

www.ingramcontent.com/pod-product-compliance
Lightning Source LLC
Chambersburg PA
CBHW060306290526
45789CB00001B/415